CHUCK CLOSE

CHUCK CLOSE

LISA LYONS AND ROBERT STORR

RIZZOLI
NEW YORK

First published in the United States of America in 1987
by RIZZOLI INTERNATIONAL PUBLICATIONS, INC.
597 Fifth Avenue
New York, NY 10017

Library of Congress Cataloging-in-Publication Data

Storr, Robert.
  Chuck Close.

  Bibliography: p. 179.
  1. Close, Chuck, 1940–   —Criticism and interpretation. 2. Photo-realism—
United States. 3. Realism in art—United States. 4. United States—Biography—
Portraits. I. Lyons, Lisa. II. Title.
N6537.C54S76 1987   709′.2′4   86-43193
ISBN 0-8478-0808-4

c \

Designed by Betty Binns Graphics
Set in type by Rainsford Type, Ridgefield, Connecticut
Printed and bound in Hong Kong
ISBN 0–8478–0808–4

CONTENTS

CHUCK CLOSE

REALISM AND ITS DOUBLES

ROBERT STORR

IN 1859 the first Salon of Photography opened at the Palais de l'Industrie. It had been thirty-seven years since Joseph Nicéphore Niepce first fixed a light-generated image to a chemically treated plate and some twenty years since Louis-Jacques-Mandé Daguerre had perfected his technique for the mass production of photographic images and made its name, the "daguerreotype," a household word. Thus, already alerted to the emergence of this new medium, Paris flocked to the 1959 show to witness and debate the evidence of photography's vaunted powers. And, although segregated from the precincts reserved for the regular Salon of Painting and Sculpture in order that a clear distinction between this scientific novelty and the traditional fine arts be maintained, the exhibition nonetheless constituted the first recognition, by the overseers of French culture, of the advent of a new technological era and of a distinctly modern mimesis.[1]

But, this initial attempt to mark an aesthetic if not physical boundary between the fine and applied arts proved futile. Dubbed "The Pencil of Nature" by William Henry Fox Talbot, the British inventor of the paper-negative process called the "calotype"—which, unlike its contemporary the "daguerreotype," was characterized by a tonal subtlety similar to that valued at the time in landscape painting—photography's artistic potential was too obvious to be ignored. Indeed, given its speed, exactitude, and ostensible neutrality of vision, photography promised to alter radically the terms of the aesthetic debate among nineteenth-century artists over the relation between "ideal" and "natural" form, posing a direct challenge to both the stilted Neoclassicism of the Academy and the heavy-handed Realism of Gustave Courbet. "One must be of one's time," declared Honoré Daumier, the cartoonist, sometime painter, and close friend of photographer Félix Nadar. Suddenly, it seemed as if the solution to this problem might lie outside the laborious disciplines of the studio, however conceived. Rather, the photograph represented a miraculous mirror on which "reality" had only to imprint itself. All of the visible world now offered itself as subject matter to this apparently objective glass "eye"—one that not only guaranteed that the resulting image would be an indelible record of its historical time, but also of a precise, if fleeting, moment.

Yet, it was not a conservative academician but Charles Baudelaire, France's first great modernist poet and critic, who was to pronounce the most severe judgment on this novelty. Arguing that at most photography offered the painter only an additional tool for study—Eugene Delacroix, whom he championed as the exemplary modern painter, eagerly used photographs as source for drawings—Baudelaire refused to accept what others presumed to be a fortuitous coincidence of technological invention and artistic advancement. "Photography," Baudelaire admonished, "must return to its true duty, which is that of handmaid to the arts and sciences, like printing and shorthand, which have neither created nor supplemented literature."[2] "Poetry and progress," he warned, "are two ambitious gentlemen that hate each other with an instinctive hatred, and when they meet along a pathway, one or the other must give way."[3] For Baudelaire the mundane modernity of bourgeois life was unbearable. The only salvation lay in the transcendental power of the imagination as revealed in the infinite variety of desire or in visions of an impossibly voluptuous realm "beyond this world." Consequently, although his portrait appears in paintings by both Courbet and Henri Fantin-Latour, Baudelaire was generally unsympathetic to Realism, rejecting the notion that a vital alternative to the sterile formulas of the Academy could be found by rendering the actual or the average. Quite the opposite; the Baudelairian artist was not a "looker" but a seer, perpetually on watch for the exceptional and the fantastic. Hence, ridiculing the public for its obsession with the mere verisimilitude and its corresponding fascination with the rigid portraiture of Daguerre, Baudelaire greeted the invention of photography and the Salon of 1859 with contempt, observing that, "From that moment onwards, our loathsome society rushed like Narcissus to contemplate its trivial image on the metallic plate."[4]

It can only be expected that Baudelaire would have regarded the faces at once monumental and emphatically banal which stare out from the work of Chuck Close with the utmost dismay. For they embody the complete, even nightmarish fulfillment of his worst fears of an art predicated upon the rapt, self-reflexive gaze of the common man. With only a relative handful of paintings, graphics, and Polaroid prints based on an even more restricted number of primary images, Close has, in fact, taken a position in the by now century-old struggle between photography and painting that is the very antithesis of Baudelaire's. Methodically fixing and inventively recasting the likeness of his anonymous and unprepossessing subjects in a gradual accumulation of kindred images, Close has developed an aesthetic in direct defiance of the assumptions regarding the primacy of the poetic imagination cherished by Baudelaire and the modernist tradition whose critical defender or mentor he has been.

This does not mean, however, that by simple formal interpolation

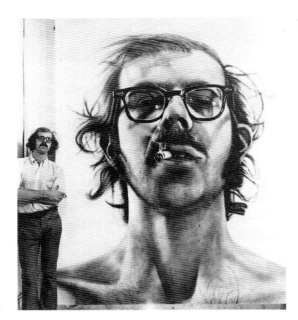

The artist with **SELF-PORTRAIT, 1968**

Close can now be inserted into art history as a latter-day practitioner of the prosaic nineteenth-century Realism Baudelaire so abhorred. Unlike those painters, past or present, who have used the camera merely to generate images that would provide their pictorial fictions with a factual alibi, Close has not exploited photography uncritically. Quite the contrary. More consistently than any artist of his generation, Close has sought to narrow if not abolish the gap between painting and photography. In so doing he has disregarded the metaphysical or humanist values habitually associated with the former. Yet he has been no less assiduous in his investigation of the status of the photograph itself and the objectivity it is supposed to represent. Furthermore, to the extent that his work may finally legitimately be considered an extension of the historical enterprise of Realism, Close's reductive techniques, limited repertoire of subjects, and constant revision and reuse of both nonetheless constitute a purposeful deconstruction and exhaustion of the inherited formal procedures and ideological premises of representational art. While it is almost certain, then, that he would have hated the paintings themselves, Baudelaire could not have failed to acknowledge—and might even have appreciated—the perversity of Close's stubbornly literal approach. And, inasmuch as Close presents a challenge to the aesthetics and epistemology of traditional Realism, it is a challenge that Charles Baudelaire and, from a very different perspective, many contemporary postmodern artists and critics, would welcome.

For most of history, painting and sculpture have, to a greater or lesser extent, been predicated on the representation of forms found in nature. Modernism constitutes a rupture with that mimetic tradition. From the disjunctive pictorial syntax of Dada and the amorphous protoplasms of Surrealism through the explosive abstraction of Wassily Kandinsky and pure geometry of Piet Mondrian and Kazimir Malevich, various tendencies have charted the progressive dissolution of the recognizable image. In its stead was promised a glimpse of worlds that lay behind or beyond appearances. By the second half of the twentieth century the philosophical or poetic visions articulated by these early modernists had been replaced by a new aesthetic materialism, which not only called into question the legitimacy of depiction, but also challenged figurative art's claim to a greater factual specificity. Viewed by its partisans as the necessary historical culmination of the Modernist search for art's essence, Formalist abstraction of the postwar era proposed an emphatically concrete Realism in which painting and sculpture, reduced to a statement of their fundamental physical and procedural properties, were representative of themselves alone.

It is not given, however, that one accept this development as either preordained or conclusive. As the critic Linda Nochlin has pointed out, the struggle between Formalism and Realism in modern times recapitulates an age-old philosophical debate which antedates by millenia the appearance of pure abstraction.[5] The original protagonists were Aristotle, for whom the natural world was, in a sense, an open book whose full meaning could be grasped through careful study, and Plato, who maintained that phenomenal reality itself was only a faint and distorted projection of a higher and more essential order. For Aristotle, knowledge, including aesthetic apprehension, was empirical; for Plato it was analytical, a matter of deducing the immutable *a priori* truths implicit but only indirectly perceived in contingent facts. While Aristotle advocated the careful imitation of natural forms, even ugly ones, as a branch of higher learning, Plato viewed the refinement of naturalistic painting and sculpture as culminating in ever-more specific and therefore imperfect simulacra of the ideal forms intended, hence the low regard in which he held poetry and the mimetic arts.

Western art has been conditioned by the dialectic between these two basic epistemological and aesthetic ideologies. Michelangelo's desperate attempts to discover and liberate the vital and transcendent forms he thought were imprisoned in the material reality of stone was a direct reflection of the Neoplatonic thinking of his time. Alberti, and the Renaissance painters who followed his lead, believed that the laws of perspective were a reflection of a divine formal harmony. The pursuit of eternal "beauty" based on mathematical systems of human proportion—systems which served as the pedagogical basis of the great European academies from the seventeenth through the nineteenth centuries—was a still further expression of such normative aesthetics. But as serene, otherworldly and exquisitely balanced as the paintings of Piero della Francesca may be, or as anguished as Michelangelo's frescos and abraded late sculptures, the work of several of their equally gifted contemporaries reflects a scientific inquisitiveness fundamentally at odds with such idealism.

His paintings may manifest an unrivaled formal perfection, but Leonardo da Vinci's notebooks, to take an obvious example, are replete with detailed anatomical, meteorological, and mechanical studies expressive of his unrelenting curiosity about the material world and how things worked. For Leonardo, drawing was dissection and what he discovered behind appearances was not just spirit but gears, veins, and physical dynamism. So too, despite his determination to assimilate the conventions of Italian Renaissance painting, Albrecht Dürer remained more of a naturalist than a classicist, stopping on his pilgrimage south to draw fallen birds or clumps of grass, integrating into his religious tableaux a host of morphological studies, and accommodating into his manual on the geometry of the figure a wealth of double chins and puckered knees.

Indeed, the Northern tradition, within which Dürer occupies a dominant position, was consistently Realist in its aesthetic preference. From van Eyck's altarpiece *The Adoration of the Lamb*, whose pastoral setting constitutes a veritable herbal in which dozens of species of flowers are carefully described, through the work of Baroque masters such as the landscapist Jacob van Ruisdael, who watched skies like an anxious hitchhiker, still-life and genre painters such as the two Bruegels and the great portraitists Rembrandt van Rijn, Frans Hals, and Anthony van Dyke, Netherlandish painting has regularly found its inspiration in cataloguing the inexhaustible variousness of quotidian reality. Even the remote and preternaturally still paintings of Jan Vermeer are as impressive for the miracle of their naturalistic luminosity as much as for the intricacy of their allegorical programs. Likewise, following the lead of Michelangelo Merisi da Caravaggio, the most radical artist of the Italian Counter Reformation, Spanish Baroque painters, including Diego Velasquez, Francesco de Zurbaran, and José Ribiera, were consistently Realist in their treatment of both portraiture and sacred and secular narratives.

From the beginning of the eighteenth century through the late nineteenth century—that is, during the very period in which the idealist conventions of the academies held greatest sway—Realism flourished as never before in the work of Jean Baptiste Chardin as well as in the topographical watercolors of English artists Paul Sandby, Thomas Girtin, and John Sell Cotman, and in oil paintings and sketches of John Constable. Even J. M. W. Turner, whose early work incorporated the Arcadian decors of Claude Lorrain and whose late paintings announced an apocalyptic Romanticism, spent much of his time sketching the English countryside or studying the play of the sun in interior spaces, exercises that informed the subject matter and chromatic exactitude of his work fully as much as they did his poetic vision. In Turner's paintings light and the forces of nature consume both the relics of the Golden Age and the dynamos of the Machine Age, while in Constable's, modesty before humble subject matter was an heroic stance and the mark of a rare visual avidity. And, despite the obvious differences in temperament and intent of the two artists, the work of both anticipates the perceptual naturalism of Impressionism.

By the mid-nineteenth century, Gustave Courbet had begun to paint bulky nymphs and vernacular tableaux, such as the *Funeral at Ornans*, that represented a direct assault on the patrician canons of the Beaux-Arts. In the 1860s, Edgar Degas, though a political conservative and disciple of the supreme academician Ingres, embarked on a course no less far-reaching in its aesthetic implications than that of his revolutionary-minded elder, Courbet. Abandoning the historical conceits of his apprentice works in favor of contemporary street scenes, candid views of the brothel and night-club life, and glimpses from behind the scenes of the theater world, Degas pioneered the use of the freeze-frame effects and eccentric cropping of photography. Finally, in the paintings of Edouard Manet, stock classical compositions, often prosaic subject matter, and a curious lack of interpretive affect were fused in a mixture that continues to prompt argument between Realists and those for whom painting is the sum of its impurities, and others for whom Manet's achievement represents the first demonstration of the disinterested purity of vision that is the goal of modern Formalism.

As should be readily apparent from this cursory review, Realism has not been the object or standard of academic aesthetics, but rather its perpetual antithesis. As such, Realism is not merely an obsolete or retrograde "style" to be superseded, but an enduring tendency inextricably woven into the fabric of Modernist thinking. If, as Linda Nochlin has said, Realism is "the criminal to the abstract law," with abstraction being the contemporary equivalent of earlier normative modes of expression, then abstraction is by the same token unthinkable without the existence of Realism as its dialectical opposite.[6] Realism is, indeed, the variable but persistent aesthetic enterprise whose negation has served as the point of departure for defining the absolutes posited by abstraction. That abstractionists constantly reiterate that difference is a grudging recognition of Realism's staying power, one that derives from a comprehensive world view and transcends issues of stylistic popularity—there have been many Realisms, and most at their inception were scorned by public tastemakers. The very objections raised against Realism by its adversaries are, in fact, an index of its professed aims and specific virtues. As Nochlin has written, "Realism has always been criticized by its adversaries for its lack of selectivity, its inability to distill from the random plenitude of experience the generalized harmony of plastic relations, as though this were a flaw rather than the *whole point of the realist strategy*."[7]

Yet, despite the long and frequently radical tradition to which it refers, in the modern era the term Realism has degenerated into a vague and usually pejorative epithet applied to virtually any form of representational painting. This habit of defining Realism simply as the antithesis of abstraction is not the fault of abstractionists alone. Too often the very artists who set out to vindicate Realism are those most guilty of such indiscriminate usage, and some have positively relished the reactionary rhetoric with which the Realist cause has become entangled. For example, Thomas Hart Benton, an expatriate abstractionist in the 1920s turned Buckeye Mannerist during the 1930s, spent the greater part of his career railing against the absurdity of nonobjective painting, at the same time discreetly acknowledging and taking pride in the genius of his prodigal artistic son, Jackson Pollock. Cramming his technicolor cartoons with icons of Depression-era Americana, Benton may have intended to be a social historian. At best, in fact, he was a folklorist. On the other hand, Precisionist painters, such as Charles Sheeler and Ralston Crawford, though contemporary in their choice of factories and urban architecture as their subject matter, and Modernist in the austere geometry of their style, found it equally hard to sustain their vision within a rigorously Realist aesthetic. Crawford followed Stuart Davis's path toward a blocky, often-decorative abstraction in which only emblematic vestiges of his machine-age motives survived. Sheeler, who used photographs as the basis of austere documentary paintings in the early 1920s, by the 1950s was making complex, synthetic Cubist compositions with the aspect of double exposures. Meanwhile, Charles Burchfield, a painter of bleak industrial scenes during the mid-1930s, in his later work veered off toward an extravagantly Gothic pastoral pantheism.

Of the American Scene painters and their immediate heirs, only Edward Hopper upheld the basic tenets of Realism, only his work succeeded in being both evocative and apparently matter of fact, timeless and always on time. The perennial exception to the general distaste for Realism expressed by the advocates of avant-garde art in the period between the two World Wars—*House by the Railroad* was the first painting by an American artist purchased by Alfred H. Barr for the Museum of Modern Art in New York—Hopper's work enjoyed an ambiguous prestige much like that afforded Edouard Manet's. Informed by prudent voyeurism and a self-effacing melancholy, it evoked the spirit of a native Existentialism, acknowledging, as it did, the ubiquity of the archetypal "lonely American." But Hopper's true isolation was aesthetic as well as psychological. For all their poetic accessibility, his hauntingly prosaic street scenes and arid interiors remained essentially inimitable. Nor did he attempt to codify and teach the principles that guided him. The only great Realist painter of his day, Hopper died with many admirers but no significant followers.

With the end of World War II, the stand-off between the American Scene painters and indigenous modernists was broken. After 1945, it was no longer possible to argue that a distinctively American painting depended on an identifiably American subject matter and so could only be Realist, however loosely that term might be applied. Having fully assimilated and fundamentally transformed the European influences upon which it had drawn, Abstract Expressionism had become the dominant tendency of the international avant-garde. Henceforth, anyone attempting to renew or reinvent representational art had first to come to terms with the example set by the New York School. For a time it appeared as if figurative painting in general would forever be playing catch-up with abstraction. Meanwhile, Realism in particular all but disappeared under an ocean of viscous pigment.

On the West Coast, his efforts seconded by mentor David Park and contemporaries Paul Wonner and Elmer Bischoff, Richard Diebenkorn combined the liquid draftsmanship he had learned from Willem de Kooning and the saturated color with the flat spatial compositions of Pierre Bonnard and Henri Matisse in a lushly chromatic suburban intimism. For all his considerable virtuosity, however, Diebenkorn's gift was for seductive compromise rather than for a rigorous revision of the figurative conventions. The poses of his figures recall those found in Hopper's static domestic scenes, but they are not so much individual presences (the description of whose unique traits and situation took precedence over all other concerns) as they were mannequins on which to hang a variety of painterly effects. In the work of another Californian, Nathan Oliveira, as in that of numerous other artists around the country, the lesson of Alberto Giacometti's return to the discipline of direct observational painting from the model was similarly misunderstood or obscured. Rather than being the consequence of an obsessive and ever more economical note-taking, as they were in Giacometti's work, the wraithlike figures in Oliveira's paintings were literary "signs" affixed to a wall of pigment covered by a heavy patina of febrile graffiti.

Presented in various biennials at the Whitney Museum of American Art and heralded in numerous theme shows, such as the Museum of Modern Art's *New Images of Man* (which, along with the paintings and sculptures of Giacometti, featured the work of Diebenkorn, Oliveira, and still more conservative artisans of angst such as Leonard Baskin), the new figuration of the late 1950s and early 1960s was thus less an alternative to Abstract Expressionism than an effort to humanize its violence and stylize its formal inventions and so subordinate them to established moral or pictorial ends. Content to borrow rather than steal the fire of the gods, these representational but scarcely Realist artists proved to be remarkably deferential "criminals" to the "abstract law."

The early 1960s, however, saw the coming together of a group of painters who were to lay the groundwork for a true resurgence of Realism in the coming decade. Although these artists were personally close to the members of the first and second generations of the New York School, that proximity seemed to reinforce their resolve to move away from, instead of toward, the hermetic symbolism and unrehearsed gesture typical of Abstract Expressionism. Painting from life rather than out of their imaginations, they addressed themselves to the most commonplace and the least dramatic aspects of contemporary reality with a marked and, to many people, disturbing psychological detachment. Not only did these artists reject the mythic ambitions of Action Painting, they addressed themselves to its formal problems as well, arriving through direct observation at a reconstitution of the fragmented image resulting from the progressive dissection and dismemberment of tangible reality begun with Impressionism and continued through Cubism, Surrealism, and their variants in postwar abstraction.

Fairfield Porter, the oldest of these new Realists, predicated his work on the deliberately anachronistic but in his case fecund premise that rather than pursuing Paul Cézanne's path toward an art of ever-increasing rarification and analytic formality, Modernism might better have followed the example of Edouard Vuillard's accepting and affectionate regard for the serendipitous confusion and evanescent delights of domestic life. Combining Vuillard's patchwork pictorial design with the limpid naturalism of Velázquez and the painterly fluency of Porter's close friend de Kooning without relying on any of these precedents for the mood or authority of his work, Porter painted a composite portrait of the extended family he headed and the comings and goings of its artist and poet members in his houses in Maine and Long Island. Unapologetically plain, the originality of his work derives from its singular immediacy of atmosphere, incident, and painterly mark. In the formulation of his aesthetic, Porter looked backward more often than forward, yet, his objective, as is evident in the paintings themselves, was to live unconditionally in the present.

While Porter's vignettes evoke a kind of Yankee *gemütlichkeit*, Alex Katz's paintings—populated by some of the same art-world personalities—are stylishly cool advertisements for the "Good Life." Drastically abbreviating essential details of gesture, likeness, and ambience in tiny cut-paper collages and painted studies, Katz then blows up these sketches to fill billboard-size canvases. Hoping to make figurative paintings that would pack the visual wallop of Franz Kline's bold structural abstractions while at the same time accenting the decorousness of the milieu he frequents and depicts, Katz superimposes flat images on flat grounds, producing bland but monumental emblems of the comforts and the conviviality of bourgeois society. A dauntingly well-mannered genre painter, Katz is a Realist by virtue of the acuity with which he monitors and records the often faint vital signs and ever-changing fashions of a world in which surface *is* substance.

The most radical and, after Porter, the most articulate of the new Realists, however, is Philip Pearlstein. After struggling for several years to make landscape paintings in a contemporary allover style, by the early 1960s Pearlstein had become one of the most severe critics of such attempts to reconcile the deep space of observational painting with the flat space of abstraction. In "Figure Paintings Today Are Not Made in Heaven," an article published in *Art News* in 1962, Pearlstein took his stand against the painterly clichés of the "Schools" of Giacometti, de Kooning, and Pollock and, more important, against the roving viewpoint of Cézanne, which had initiated the gradual disappearance of integrated volumetric form in modern painting. Affirming that the task of the Realist painter consisted of nothing more or less than the scrupulous transcription of things seen, Pearlstein posed his life models in interiors bereft of all but the most utilitarian studio props and painted them with a merciless attentiveness to the imperfections of their bodies and a startling indifference to their psychological presence. An empiricist and autodidact, Pearlstein ignored the suave formulas of the academic rear-guard as assiduously as he avoided accommodation with the prevailing ideology of the Tenth Street avant-garde, mak-

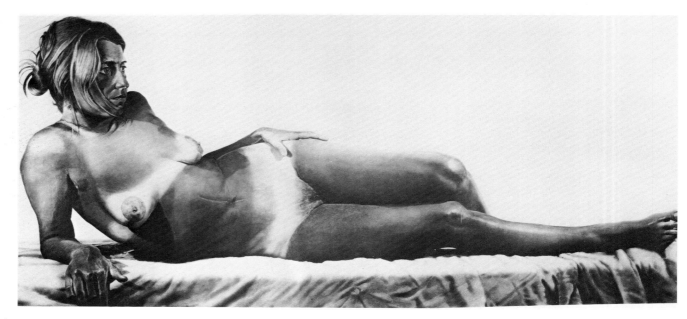

ing paintings that were the most uncompromising and at the same time most uningratiating figure paintings to appear since those of Thomas Eakins.

Thus, by the time that Chuck Close entered the Graduate School of Art and Architecture at Yale in 1962, a fundamental re-examination of the working assumptions of de Kooning, Rothko, Kline, and Pollock was already well under way. Further evidence of this change was to be found in the emergence of Pop art, and Color Field and Hard-Edge Abstraction. And although the prevailing beginner's style among students of the period remained quasi-Expressionist, that reflex was meeting serious challenges from progressive as well as conservative instructors in the art conservatories.

Among the most influential figures at Yale at the time was Josef Albers, an unapologetic academician, arch anti-Romantic, and vigilant adversary of the happy—or rather profoundly unhappy—accidents upon which the aesthetics of Abstract Expressionism had been based. As ascerbic as Ad Reinhardt, the other ardent debunker of the Expressionist mystique, it was Albers who took it upon himself in the mid-1960s to send critic Harold Rosenberg a telegram informing him matter-of-factly that "angst is dead." As demonstrated in his didactic series of paintings *Homage to the Square* and his Bauhaus pedagogy, Albers was the relentless defender of an art based on frank intentionality and pure perception. Although Albers had officially retired before Close arrived at Yale, his impact on the art department persisted. To study there was to contend with his immediate legacy as much as with the more distant authority of the New York School of painting. Thus, directly through his own teaching or indirectly through that of his former students who remained on the faculty, Albers served as the guide or nemesis to several generations of artists who passed through New Haven, artists as diverse in sensibility as Eva Hesse, Richard Serra, Robert Mangold, Nancy Graves, and Brice Marden. Moreover, despite the strict nonobjectivity of his work, Albers's methodical approach to painting exerted a considerable influence on the active group of Realist painters who emerged from Yale in the 1950s and 1960s, one that, in addition to Close, included Neil Welliver, Sylvia Plimack Mangold, Janet Fish, John Moore, and Rackstraw Downes, a landscapist whose apparently fisheye lens but in actuality directly observed perspectives contrast instructively with the flatness of Close's portraits.

However, it was neither Albers's dogmas, which Close felt were outdated, that convinced him of the futility of trying to emulate the

Abstract Expressionists, nor the example of Realist painters then at Yale: Pearlstein, Katz, Welliver (formerly Albers's teaching assistant), and William Bailey. In fact, Close studied with Jack Tworkov, whose paintings during his tenure evolved from a lacerated biomorphism akin to that of his former studio mate de Kooning toward a kind of gestural grid painting. Rather, what undermined Close's faith in his own attempts at Action Painting was the facility with which he could mimic a style whose authenticity and entire philosophical rationale resided in struggle. Angst, or its appearance, was not so much "dead" as it was "easy." The irony of this realization was made all the more disconcerting when Philip Guston, a visiting artist at Yale, singled out one of Close's paintings for special mention. The effect on Close was profound. For although he tried in vain to make another painting as strong, he became increasingly aware of his capacity to make paintings that were "almost" convincing. If taste could thus approximate the decisions supposedly dictated by metaphysical necessity, what then remained of the ethos of Abstract Expressionism?

Like the School of Paris recipes that it had so radically revised, New York School painting had in turn become a kind of painterly "haute cuisine." It was, furthermore, just one of many offerings on the scholastic menu. Chance, in the form of the university computer, might just as well have placed him in "Painting Class 101 instead of 102," Close recalled, where he would have "started making paintings with masking tape" and in revolt against that "perhaps I would have ended up making thick, loose, open paintings."[8] A precocious technician, Close's problem was thus the classic one of a gifted student who, capable of doing anything, cannot settle on a reason for doing anything in particular.

The answer for Close was not to be found in the eventual discovery of an "inner necessity," but on the contrary, in a wholesale surrender to "outward" appearance and the revelation that the least of aesthetic "ideas" could paradoxically result in the most complex painterly results. Even as he continued to make abstractions for the remainder of his time as a graduate student, his first mature work after leaving Yale was a huge painting of a woman measuring 10 by 22 feet. Based on a photograph and executed in color in a 1965 version and in black and white in a second 1967 version, these two nudes were less a transition than a plunge into Realism. Immediately, Close faced basic problems in the format and imagery of these paintings, the solution of which has determined the constants of his work since that time.

JUD (profile), 1981

Wanting to make a Realist image comparable in impact, scale, and allover structure to an abstraction by Frank Stella or Jackson Pollock, Close was forced to concede that his subject matter and the average viewer's psychological responses to it undermined the non-hierarchical reading of the figure he intended. A nude, Close realized, has "hot spots" which almost inevitably distract attention and so prevent a disinterested examination of the picture as a fully integrated entity. At the same time, despite the vast dimensions of the canvas, Close found himself limited in the amount of detail he could accommodate in any given part of the painting. The answer, he decided, was to concentrate on a part of the body rather than the whole, and to choose one that did not permit a reflex reading. Thus, with the recent exception of his over-life-size and sexually detailed but erotically neutral Polaroids of naked men and women, and occasional profile portraits such as *Jud*, 1981, from this point onward Close has taken the frontally posed head as his exclusive starting point.

In many respects Close's approach to the problems of Realism parallels that of Pearlstein. Both artists have sought to treat the figure with an utter matter-of-factness and have as a result been confronted with the charge that their objectivity fails to respect the inherent humanity of their subject matter. Both artists have chosen fidelity to fact as the dialectical counterforce to their underlying preoccupation with pictorial structure. To that extent their work is as much formal, though not in the contemporary sense Formalist, as it is realistic. Finally, both Pearlstein and Close have rejected the idea dear to the Abstract Expressionists that a painting is never finished but only abandoned. While the Expressionists maintained that specific works of art were in a sense the byproducts of a vital impulse that transcended the object in which it was briefly invested, Pearlstein and Close have adhered to the premise that the integrity of a painting depends upon its completion. That is to say the exhaustive transcription of all of the information contained in the given reality from which they work. Seeking to take full account of what is knowable rather than to evoke essences which must always remain mysterious, they create paintings in which the final appearance is explicit in the subject matter they choose and the procedures they employ.

As instructive as these parallels may be, there are, nevertheless, some crucial distinctions to be made. The most important is that whereas Pearlstein works from life, varying the poses of his models from painting to painting, Close works from photographs in which the image has already been synthesized and fixed within a flat pictorial format. Further, if Pearlstein's carefully orchestrated variations on his basic set-up and his very awkwardness as a painter have insured against mere redundancy, Close's limited choice of source material and his manual facility have largely denied him that freedom. What remains is the variety that results from a total concentration on rendering the atomized visual detail made available and transformed by technical manipulation of the image. Pearlstein has struggled to reconcile the anomalies of perspective and scale created by the unassisted eye as it attempts to encompass and rationalize three-dimensional reality; Close has investigated the details and structure of an image frozen by the camera's monocular vision.

This resort to a static photographic image—which has provided Close with an infinitely patient and inexpensive model—has correspondingly meant the virtual effacement of the painter as the primary perceptual protagonist of the work. As indifferent to the phenomenological contingency of his own direct experience of nature as he has been to the psychology of his models or the ethical imperatives of traditional figure painting, Close has all but absented himself from the picture. Both he and his photographic motives are but vestigial specters of a once-dynamic relation between painter and model. This may seem to some a dubious achievement, but inasmuch as stylistic transparency—a close equivalence between model and artifact—is the ultimate aim of hard-core Realism, Close, by reducing the artist's role to that of a meticulous scanning agency, has realized that goal with a singular completeness.

It is by virtue of this detachment and the artist's emphasis on the independent, epistemological status of his source material that Close's paintings distinguish themselves most decisively from the raft of Photo Realist work that appeared in the late 1960s and early 1970s. For the most part, other Photo Realists of the period seemed content to use the camera to supply themselves with an intrinsically evocative subject matter, ignoring, except on the most superficial level, the peculiar characteristics and conditions of the photographic image. The snapshot, as Baudelaire had long ago warned, was simply being used as a shortcut toward an ever-more refined but pedestrian illusionism. Too often, in fact, Photo Realist painting constituted little more than a demonstration of craftsmanship, though in the work of Richard Estes, whose paintings display the proficiency of a Beaux-Arts valedictorian, there is a technical mastery that is hard to dismiss.

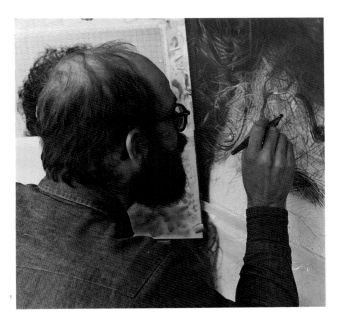

Left: Artist at work in studio
Right: **DICK, 1981,** detail

Photo Realism was just as conservative in its approach to its vernacular muse as it was in its formal strategies. Relying for their meaning on the public's immediate and presumably amused or sympathetic recognition of the icons they incorporated, burger palaces, chrome-heavy Harley Davidsons, and Woolworth's knick-knacks, the majority of Photo Realist paintings simply cultivated a nostalgia for the present. Taking cues from Pop art, while for the most part dispensing with the subversive ironies that initially gave the work of Roy Lichtenstein, Edward Ruscha, Claes Oldenburg, and other aficionados of the commercial culture its edge, or imitating the design conventions of Hard-Edge Abstraction and supergraphics, Photo Realism as a tendency accomplished little more than a hi-tech gloss on various other contemporary styles, producing not so much a "new" Realism as an updated version of 1930s Regionalism as instantly dated as the hope of finding your "kicks" on Route 66.

Close's approach to photography, however, has always been as much critical as instrumental. Correspondingly, although it is inevitable that critics would describe him as a Photo Realist, Close has frequently expressed his discomfort at an association with the movement. Indeed, given the analytic- or process-oriented nature of his aesthetic, Close more appropriately belongs in the company of Minimalist or systems artists, such as Sol LeWitt, Nancy Graves, and Richard Serra.

Like LeWitt's, Close's work is equational rather than improvisational. Both artists begin by clearly setting forth the formal premises that will govern the creation of a given piece, rules then followed to the letter (unlike LeWitt, who delegates the execution of his wall drawings to assistants and has his sculptures commercially fabricated, Close is the sole author of his paintings). There is no mystification of process. Form is the product of formulas, not inspiration. The function of the artist is the *real*-ization or *object*-ification of a working hypothesis.

Meanwhile, just as Serra adumbrated his mature work by first composing a list of primary materials and the basic sculptural operations, Close set out to define for himself the simplest means available for making a painting and the simplest technical procedures for employing them. In practice, this at first meant restricting himself to thin black pigment applied over a white ground. Subsequently, in his color paintings, Close limited himself to an equally reductive palette of the same three primary red, blue, and yellow hues. Applying water-based colors with an airbrush, daubing inks with his fingers, grinding dry pastel pigments into the fabric of

rough papers, collaging tonally modulated chips of paper pulp, experimenting with a number of etching processes, and finally making large-format photographs with a prototype camera developed by Polaroid, Close has varied his production so that it constitutes an inventory of basic methods for placing an image on a flat surface. In each endeavor he isolates and analyzes the inherent properties of various media he employs. The object of this exercise is not just to make a picture but to lay bare what a picture is made of.

The artist of Close's generation whose concerns most nearly approximate his own, however, is Nancy Graves. In her filmmaking, painting, and multifaceted sculptural practice, Graves too has made technical experimentation and technical virtuosity a primary focus for her energies. Her part in reviving bronze casting and polychroming in a period when such supposedly antiquated crafts were scorned by many contemporary sculptors corresponds to Close's interest in mezzotint, a long-neglected printing medium. A more fundamental affinity lies in their mutual determination to integrate aesthetic and scientific inquiry. Graves's early work, for example, consisted of a careful study of the morphology of the camel. In a protracted series of works that ranged from assemblages and Minimalist scatter pieces to fully articulated figures of camels that seemed a kind of inspired taxidermy, Graves explored the tension between abstract invention and precise, even pedantic reproduction, the part and the whole, the typical structure of natural forms and the unique embodiment of those structures as found in individual specimens. As do Close's paintings, Graves's works manifest a straightforward inquisitiveness about the information that can be deduced from organic forms when approached not as "found objects" to be assimilated by a preexisting aesthetic practice but as self-sufficient and self-generating "found systems" that art making, by effacing itself, can elucidate.

If the development of Close's paintings was in this way determined by the gradually revealed complexity of his chosen image, it was no less dictated by the axioms of the pictorial system within which the information the image yielded was to be charted. That system was the grid. The essential formal and philosophical construct of modern art from Cubist abstraction through the Minimalism of the 1960s and 1970s, its evolution is most succinctly summarized in the work of Piet Mondrian. From his early dunescapes, quasi-abstract depictions of church towers and willows, and the floating axes of his "plus-minus" works to the spare armatures of his Neoplasticist paintings of the 1920s onward, one can trace in

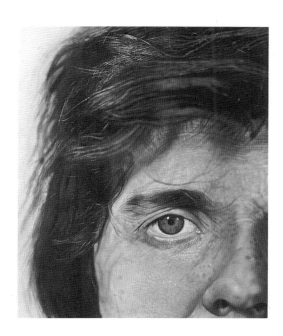

Mondrian's art the slow birth of the depthless planar space that is the hallmark of the modern abstraction. With the emergence of the grid, the surface of a painting became a field over which essentially two-dimensional marks and shapes are distributed rather than a capacious void within which to project an illusion of the visible, tactile world.

The fundamental unit of any pictorial grid is derived from the proportions of the given canvas, the placement of each formal element by the artist either reinforcing or revising the implicit reticulated template arrived at by the mathematical division of that primary rectangle. In Mondrian's paintings, intuitively arrived-at asymmetrical arrangements of verticals and horizontals are opposed to the basic symmetry of the formats, revealing a dynamic equilibrium the artist considered the most elemental and profound aesthetic experience. Many contemporary painters, however, have tended to reiterate rather than tamper with that inherent symmetry. In the work of Agnes Martin, for example, the structures superimposed by the artist constitute a patient insistence on the regularity of the painting's intrinsic matrix. In this way, scored in equal intervals, space within the grid is perfectly balanced and inviolable. It is to the inorganic nature and the ideal orderliness of such space that the grid owes its claim to a metaphysical or, conversely, a utopian materialistic supremacy; such claims have informed the teleological aesthetics of everyone from Mondrian and Malevich through American Formalists inspired by critics such as Clement Greenberg. For them the discovery of grid and the corresponding flatness of picture plane marked the end of the mimetic tradition.

Yet such conclusions are neither historically nor formally inevitable. For if, in Modernist painting, the grid has been the emblem of a progressive divorce between art and the natural world, historically it might equally be seen as the primary agency responsible for the assimilation of the latter by the former. Indeed, since the Renaissance, the grid has been a standard method for enlarging and transferring a drawing to a canvas. Rather than use an opaque projector to transpose and scale up his photographs—a procedure that would result in a blurred rather than sharply focused image—Close himself employs the grid technique.

In its most common application, the grid is a mapping device. Frequently in the past as well as the present it has been used in combination with photography. The camera obscura, a protophotographic invention that used a lens or pinhole to project images onto a darkened drawing surface, often incorporated gridded filters to facilitate the transcription process. In Eadweard Muybridge's serial photo studies of men and animals in motion—a body of work that had a profound effect on Close's friend, the composer Philip Glass, as well as many other Minimalists—the grid served to measure and organize the intervals and repetitions revealed by Muybridge's stop-action technique. More recently, in a series of paintings based on images of the earth and moon sent back by satellites, Nancy Graves has explored the dynamic relation between mapping systems and sequential photography.

Map-grids, however, flatten the relief of the three-dimensional entities they represent, as for example when a section of the globe is peeled away from its volumetric core and spread out with all topographical detail diagrammatically rendered in concentric shape-clusters. In a sense, Close treats the face as just such a topographical surface, but, within the conventional shallowness of the map-grid, he inserts a photographic image that introduces an incongruous, albeit diminished, three-dimensional illusion. For that image is informed by spatial anomalies peculiar to the photographic process. In extreme close-up the camera's depth of field can cause those features closest to the camera to become amorphous, whereas to the naked eye they would be seen with the greatest clarity. Close has actively exploited such discrepancies. In a painting such as *Kent*, 1970–71, for example, the nose and the hair at the side of the head to the back—that is, both those things farthest and nearest to the viewer—are equally hazy, while the cheek and eyes which occupy the middle ground are perfectly resolved. By the apparently simple operation of setting the conventions of the map-grid against the optical distortions of the photograph, Close has opened up a pictorial space that neither obeys the laws of traditional representational painting in which the canvas, viewed metaphorically as a window on the world, is used as the framework for a perspectival reconstruction of palpable, fully volumetric reality, nor adheres to a rationale of contemporary abstraction which disallows the intrusion of any degree of three-dimensional form into painting's two-dimensional realm. Placing his images squarely in the middle of the canvas, which they nearly fill, Close gives his paintings neither context nor composition. They contain no lines of force or space-generating diagonals that might zigzag against the axes of the implicit grid and so create an illusion of deep space. Only the subtle blur of the nose acts as repoussoir. Sandwiched between a foreground and background, which, in their comparable lack of focus, share equal status relative to the picture plane, we examine these

17

faces as if they are specimens encased between laboratory slides, the thinnest possible slivers of an organic reality isolated and vastly enlarged by technology.

This capacity for enlargement is one of the principal characteristics of photographic vision. The "close-up"—a term punned to exhaustion in the discussion of Close's work—informs the work of numerous other contemporary painters. Alex Katz, for example, regularly exploits the cropping and zoom techniques of movie montage in his work. But whereas Katz blows up his images without filling them in, Close has explored the dynamics and connotations of enlargement in two distinct but complementary ways. On the one hand, the scale of his paintings amplifies the image so that, at a distance, it confronts us with an almost overwhelming presence. On the other, by painstakingly accounting for the smallest details of form, texture, and color within the expanded field, Close's paintings invite the most careful inspection. Enthralled by this wealth of information before us, we approach the picture until it envelops us and all but the area under our direct scrutiny loses its specific dimension and clarity. The camera first projects its reality toward us, invading our space with the gigantic product of its *close-up* vision. Then, we, abandoning ourselves to curiosity, voluntarily reciprocate that action and move *close in* to the painting.

As Walter Benjamin noted in his seminal text "The Work of Art in the Age of Mechanical Reproduction," this exchange between the man and camera has unveiled a distinctly modern universe:

Fifty years ago a slip of the tongue passed more or less unnoticed. . . . Since "The Psychopathology of Everyday Life," things have changed. This book isolated and made analyzable things which had heretofore floated unnoticed in the broad stream of perception. For the entire spectrum of optical, and now acoustical, perception, the film has brought about a similar deepening of apperception. . . . By close-ups of things surrounding us, by focussing on the hidden details of familiar objects, by exploring commonplace milieus under the ingenious guidance of the camera, the film, on the one hand, extends our comprehension of the necessities which rule our lives; on the other hand, it manages to insure us of an immense and unexpected field of action. . . . Evidently a different nature opens itself to the camera than opens to the naked eye—if only because an unconsciously penetrated space is substituted for a space consciously explored by man. . . . The camera introduces us to unconscious optics as does psychoanalysis to unconscious impulses.[9]

To be sure, Close's studied neutrality prohibits any direct psychological reading of his paintings; nor does his work readily lend itself to political interpretation such as Benjamin's essay might suggest. Despite that neutrality, however, his paintings impose on us a unique, almost hallucinogenic intimacy. Looking at them triggers the claustrophobic discomfort we experience when the distance we expect to be maintained on greeting someone is not respected, and he thrusts his face forward to meet ours, impinging on our private space. By the same token, however, the privacy of Close's subjects is also violated. Indeed, these images are both startlingly immodest and startlingly frank. The oily fissures of the skin, stubble, and uneven teeth that confront us in a Close self-portrait tell us more than we may reasonably want to know in answer to the simple question, "What does he look like?" Yet Close's paintings also grant us a special license to indulge our curiosity without fear. Staring at them with the innocent indiscretion of a child, we are free to remark that there is a hair hanging from a grown-up's colossal nose.

As dispassionate about his task as he may for the most part be, Close on occasion betrays a subdued affection for his sitters. In *Fanny*, a 1985 thumbprint portrait of his grandmother-in-law, Close treats his subject as if he were caressing a familiar face, his hand leaving a distinctive organic mark that, by accumulation and a curious visual metamorphosis, becomes the delicate texture of the aged woman's skin. Nonetheless, in numerous other works in which Close has used this technique, no such interpretation is plausible. Rather, aside from its purely graphic possibilities, Close appears to have chosen it as a way of punning on the idea of "tactile values" long considered by traditional art historians to be the essential characteristic of representation. Further, by juxtaposing the insistent "handmade" quality of his mark with the "hands-off" presence of his photographic grids, and by obfuscating the uniqueness of his thumbprint through repetition and superimposition, Close nicely confuses the issues of signature style versus the anonymity toward which systems art tends—the value of the painter's touch as opposed to the presumed sterility of mechanical facture.

Fused out of thousands of marks in the case of the thumbprint paintings, and in the case of his larger airbrush grid paintings out of more than one hundred thousand bursts of dilute pigment, Close's images are realized by the steady accretion of discrete bits of information in a fashion reminiscent of Impressionism or, more specifically, of the Post-Impressionist Pointillism of Seurat. Like Seurat's, Close's incremental manner of execution is labor intensive to an extreme. Correspondingly, his production, though considerably augmented by printed editions, is exceedingly small. Painting

LINDA, 1975–76, detail
LINDA/PASTEL, 1977, detail

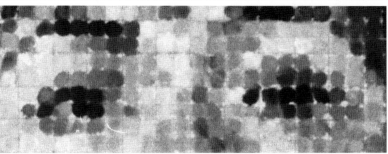

in this way becomes almost an act of endurance. This regimen directly contradicts the notion that for a painting to be interesting, the artist himself must be demonstrably "interested" or emotionally involved while he works. Indeed, Close admits that he approaches his work as if it were a job, keeping regular hours and setting himself quotas much as a professional writer would commit himself to a daily word count. Such discipline, of course, does not preclude, indeed is designed to accommodate boredom, and, as Close has noted, Seurat, no less workmanlike in his approach, must certainly have been bored as he stubbornly filled in the tiny dots that compose his masterpiece *Sunday Afternoon at La Grande Jatte*, a work that, like a Close painting, took two years to complete.

Although Close seems to share with Seurat an exaggerated fastidiousness and doggedness, the specific object of his attention is quite different. The resemblance of Close's work to Seurat's is, finally, more a matter of appearance or temperament than of substance. Seurat's obsession was with natural light. What he sought was to rationalize the perceptual divisionism of the Impressionists and to encode scientifically the spectral phenomenon of daylight falling on or reflected off forms in space. Close, by contrast, is concerned only with light and form insofar as they have already been translated by photographic and print media. He is not inventing a system to capture or analyze optical reality but replicating the effect produced by the technical processes of color separation and the dot matrix.

In *Study for Kent*, a 1970 watercolor, for example, Close exposes the means by which such mechanical processes operate. Fragmenting the face and leaving whole areas of the paper bare, Close displays the stages in which colors are overlaid to create the image. Some sections are blocked in with only a single primary color; others, reaching a greater verisimilitude, are the result of two primaries combined; and only right eye, chin, and hair above the forehead have been fully realized by the mixing of all three hues. At the bottom of the page, Close then appended color swatches that schematically lay out the mixtures he has used, making explicit the purely chromatic basis of the drawing he has created in tiny abstract paintings that contain no rendered form or texture.

As this picture demonstrates, the techniques of photo printing Close emulates compose an illusion by first decomposing the primary image they are designed to reproduce. One is thus reminded that if the grid as a planar system of equal units is infinitely expandable by the simple addition of more such units, it is, by the same token, infinitely divisible just as a line can be extended in either direction by adding points or can be broken up into even smaller fractions as points are mathematically subdivided. As a corollary, the gravitational geometry of the grid is simultaneously centripetal and centrifugal, the information it contains tending on the one hand toward entropic dispersion, on the other toward collapse and an ever-greater cohesion.

In Close's paintings, from the early black-and-white portraits, such as *Richard*, 1969, and *Nancy*, 1968, to recent full-color works such as *Leslie*, 1985–86, the implicit grid has been a fine mesh, contracting the image until it reached a hyperreal density of detail. In his prints and drawings, however, Close's grids have generally been more open and the image more etiolated. This continual expansion and contraction of the grid has had a pronounced effect on the relation of figure and ground. The looser the matrix and the softer the focus of the image, the more a face will seem to blur into the halftone of the page and so fuse with its support whereas in the tighter renderings of Close's paintings a face will seem to emerge from or float on the hard white prime of the canvas. The larger paintings are the most photographic in their resolution; in his works on paper the combined effect of the open grids and Close's graphic sleight of hand is to make sly allusions to other media. Stippled with a brush, smudged with his thumb, or hatched with a soft pencil, a given image may in one drawing have the crisp chiaroscuro of a Kodalith offset image, in another the fuzzy regularity of a computer print-out and in still another the irradiated flicker of a color television screen. Viewed together these drawings take on a kaleidoscopic interchangeability.

Altering the means and formats he employs has had quite unexpected effects upon the physiognomy of Close's subjects as well. For as the grid is enlarged and the number of units within it decreased, it becomes necessary to abbreviate the detail to be rendered. The gradual subtraction of the intermediate steps that modulate tone, form, and the nuances of structure and expression that give a face its distinctive configuration lead finally to a wholly new image. So, for example, the wary and somewhat quizzical presence which confronts us in *Phil*, 1969, becomes an almost genial countenance in many of the drawings that derive from it. In a 1977 pastel, *Linda*, eyes once steady in the 1975–76 painting of the same subject begin to waiver and cross, while the open placid face of *Mark*, 1978–79, devolves into a manic stare in subsequent watercolors. It is as if these faces were pulled and constricted in a kind

Left: **MARK, 1978–79**
Right: **MARK WATERCOLOR/UNFINISHED, 1978**

of involuntary mugging. In sequence they look back at us with the always awkward and ever-fluid personas of people seen in the four-part snapshot strips that advertise penny arcade Photomat machines.

Close must certainly recognize the humor and, in some cases, the latent anxiety found in these serial portraits. Still, such connotations are a projection neither of the subject's mood nor of the artist's own temperament. Once again, it is a manipulation of process of, not an examination of, or intentional emphasis on, human nature that accounts for the multiple readings that their alternately vulnerable, aggressive, or bemused expressions invite. Yet, cloning his images in this way, Close has managed to populate an entire world, or at any rate a small town, with individuals who, despite their inbred family resemblance, manifest a remarkable diversity of personalities.

Meanwhile, in formal terms, Close in his own fashion has found a way to solve the perennial problem posed by modernist reductivism, and most explicitly by Ad Reinhardt's late work—namely, how to make "one painting" that is at the same time not the same painting in each new version. To that end, Close has approached the head less as a unique presence to be documented than as an infinitely recyclable format. At the same time, his response to Reinhardt's dilemma incorporates the strategy of Jasper Johns. Using the face as a two-dimensional icon as Johns used flags, targets, and maps, Close in effect follows Johns's artistic credo, "Take an object. Do something to it. Do something else." Johns's art owes its subversiveness to the indifference he shows toward the intrinsic value generally imputed to the emblems he appropriates and decontextualizes. His work constitutes an oblique but devastating assault on their symbolic meaning. Close's apparently no less disinterested obsession with faces is equally challenging to conservative notions regarding the innate dignity and integrity of the figure, for the very procedures he uses to construct his images also entail their isolation and progressive deconstruction.

In this respect, Close's work anticipates the current critique of representation carried out by a host of artists now exploring the dialectic between the mass-reproduced image and the unique art object. And, if systems breed variety, mere multiplication leads to depletion. This, indeed, is one of the primary lessons of Walter Benjamin's essay "The Work of Art in the Age of Mechanical Reproduction." Traditionally, paintings have been surrounded by what he called an "aura," a metaphysical nimbus engendered by

their unique status in the realm of otherwise conventional objects. That uniqueness was a product of the exceptional nature of a painting's genesis and the particular moment and circumstances in which each viewer encountered it. In the past, for example, the *Mona Lisa* could only be known by direct experience. No description, sketch, or print could be considered an adequate surrogate for the original. In modern times, the camera and the press have undermined if not destroyed the dynamics of the encounter between a singular work and a singular individual, and with it art's "aura." In exchange for partial knowledge of an immense variety of images, we confront each at greater remove, our fundamental experience shifting, whether we know it or not, to an involvement with the technical media by means of which these images are made available to us and in the process depreciated. The sense of aesthetic immanence which once informed the act of looking at painting has vanished. As Benjamin argued,

Even the most perfect reproduction of a work of art is lacking in one element: its presence in time and space, its unique existence at the place it happens to be ... The presence of the originals is the prerequisite to the concept of authenticity. By making many reproductions, it [media technology] substitutes a plurality of copies for a unique existence.[10]

Inundated with these simulacra we lose track of the original. Now full-color copies of the *Mona Lisa* abound, including those on textured boards which ostensibly reproduce the texture of individual brushmarks in the stamped strokes that bear no relation to the surface of the actual painting. One no longer makes the pilgrimage to the Louvre in order to see the painting, but to stand in the presence of the *thing* that engendered the mass-produced *thing* that hangs over the sofa at home. In this way, for most consumers of images, the genuine work of art, reduced to a mere prototype, survives only as a remote and diminished residue within the myriad facsimiles.

In a sense the human presence preserved in Close's work is just such a residue—but not entirely. For the artist's use of technology produces curiously dichotomous results and if his graphic works document the dissolution of the image, his paintings, as has been pointed out, are in many respects more complete than the snapshots from which they derive. Hence, Close's self-imposed discipline both confirms and at the same time inverts the terms and progression of Benjamin's theoretical argument. For inasmuch as he has set himself the task of doing by hand what is supposedly done only by

machines, Close vastly enriches the photographs from which he copies. His work may lack the mystique associated with traditional figure painting, but in its place we find a wealth of "fact" that even the most faithful reproduction of Close's "reproductive" images cannot approximate.

Indeed, the irony of Close's hyper-Realist aesthetic resides precisely in its lack of irony. Here, the comparison between Close and Andy Warhol is instructive. Like Warhol, the sardonic "father" of contemporary appropriative or deconstructive art, Close seems to aspire to being a machine. But if Warhol has adopted a mechanical persona in order to underscore his contempt for art*work*, Close has labored with a diligence that, by contrast, seems the purest affirmation of the Protestant ethic. Where Warhol exposes the image as commodity simultaneously mocking and exploiting the social and aesthetic systems that accord such commercial objects privileged status and "meaning," Close, setting aside such considerations, consumes his images as a raw material in order to analyze the technical systems that engender them.

Poised near the center of recent debates over the consequences of the media's problematic symbiosis with painting, Close's work is, however, rarely mentioned in this context. Neither a polemic against nor a bland affirmation of representational prerogatives, his project is, perhaps, too self-contained to enter actively into such discussions. Given the artist's apparently apolitical stance, the restricted givens of his enterprise and his indifference to style as such—his work has signature images too indentifiable to be appropriated yet has no signature manner that might be imitated—it is difficult if not impossible to trace any direct influence of Close's work on that of other younger artists. Nevertheless the conceptual dualisms he has tested and the risks he has assumed in the programmatic generation and degeneration of images—the primary risk being a slide into the manufacture of purely decorative objects devoid of any critical necessity or visual distinction—place him in dialogue with the deconstructive or photo-appropriative artists of the 1980s. Like them, he is not concerned with the "natural" but with the "denatured" aspect of art-making. "The only way that I can accomplish what I want," Close has said, "is to understand not the reality of what I am dealing with, but the artificiality of what it is. So perhaps I would feel more comfortable with 'new artificialist' than with 'new realist'."[11]

Located within the larger "grid" of contemporary art, Close's work thus overlaps with that of the Minimal, Conceptual, and Pop artists of his generation and the Deconstructivists of recent years. At these points of congruence his paintings engage issues that Realists have for the most part ignored. The fact that they have done so explains Close's uneasy acceptance of Realist rubric. Yet finally it is upon Realism that Close's work has had the greatest and most lasting influence. For by depicting process as well as painting faces, he has opened Realism to a radical reexamination of its own formal and ideological assumptions. Despite its stated aims, Realism, no less than other more obviously "imaginative" styles, is predicated on a willing suspension of disbelief. If, in the past, strict Realists have always striven to reproduce forms objectively, as if the intervention of the artist was a disinterested act, Close make us acutely aware that objectivity is a pose. As we know from both the social and exact sciences, things can never be perceived and represented in their virtual state inasmuch as perception is always conditioned by circumstance, and representation always an intrusive and selective act. The threat presented by Close's pictorial research then is not so much to the imaginary and the ideal, as Baudelaire conceived of them, as it is to the positivist ideology from which traditional Realism derives its authority, namely the belief that "facts" constitute the immutable essence of "reality" and that by an empirical accounting of them it is possible to have complete and impartial knowledge of the world around us.

More poignantly than any Realist genre, portraiture embodies this problem of the elusive particularity of being and in no other genre has the effect of photography upon painting been more evident. As has already been noted, Degas often framed his images as if they were photographs. By so doing he emphasized the incidental nature of his subject. Each painting is a glimpse of a reality *in time*. In *Place de la Concorde*, for example, he captures the likeness of Vicomte Ludovic Lepic as a "man in the street" passing the artist's eye on his way out of the picture, rather than as a stolid "man of property" ensconced in the permanence of his home—the customary treatment in portraiture of the period. Similarly, Manet's historical tableau *The Execution of the Emperor Maximilian* in part owes its peculiar sense of moment to the documentary photographs the painter relied upon to reconstruct the scene. The American Realist Thomas Eakins also made frequent use of the camera. His portraits are at once stiff and revealing, like those made in long sittings in a nineteenth-century photographer's studio.

By taking simple head shots as his source, Close has chosen photographs of the lowest order and from them invented a painted

portraiture "degree zero." No empathy informs these pictures. Nor any satire. Close is not creating trompe-l'oeil stereotypes in the manner of Duane Hanson's epoxy sculptures of suburban housewives or working stiffs. But, acquainted only with their average-sounding first names, we have no way of knowing who these nonetheless emphatically individual people may be. We are far indeed from the stagey minimalism of Richard Avedon's portraits in which a shiver of recognition informs our delight in the grotesqueries of the "beautiful people" on display. If we have by now learned that the pugnacious character who glowers at us in *Richard* is the sculptor Richard Serra, it is a fact that subtracts from rather than adds to the image, for it is anonymity as much as specificity that accounts for the strange confrontational presence of these heads—and a certain physical remoteness as well. For, unlike Duane Hanson's life-size zombies, they do not insinuate themselves into our space as "real" people, nor, looming over us like Big Brother posters, does their glance meet ours. Rather, they are mute and unheroic beings raised to heroic proportions and frozen in a photographic present.

More than this, however, what separates us from them is the experiential fact of duration. Portrait painting is an act of collaborative concentration in which both the artist and the model willfully suspend time in order to create an image whose ultimate immediacy is a continuity of temporal fragments. In a portrait, each sitting is but a fraction of the extended "moment" the painting represents. The snapshot, however, takes only a second to make. Concentration may anticipate the image, but it is expressed as a sudden reflex. Once he has found or recognized the particular pose he is seeking, the portrait photographer does not linger. Nor, given the surfeit of such images, is one likely to linger over a picture once taken. Rather one quickly reads it to ascertain its likeness and goes on.

In Close's work the slow time of painting and the fast time of the photography are paradoxically co-extensive. On the one hand, his source images bear witness to the briefest of encounters; on the other his paintings are a product of hours of intense labor. All that seems obvious or incidental in the former is invested with an indelible complexity in the latter. The literal "subject" of his pictures can be taken in at a glance, yet one nonetheless finds oneself constantly returning to scrutinize them for new details. The duration of the viewer's participation in this contradictory exercise—an abbreviated version of the artist's own commitment to the work—represents the real time in which the paintings exist as paintings,

but it remains a duration forever alien to the photographic reality the paintings duplicate.

The irony of these conflicting temporal realities has still larger and more disturbing implications. Searching for the essential characteristic that distinguishes photography from all other mimetic techniques, Roland Barthes concluded that it was the uniqueness of the photographic instant.

What the Photograph reproduces to infinity, Barthes noted, has occurred only once: the Photograph mechanically repeats what could never be repeated existentially. In the Photograph, the event is never transcended for the sake of something else: the Photograph always leads the corpus I need back to the body I see; it is the absolute Particular, the sovereign Contingency, matte and somehow stupid.[12]

No description of Close's paintings could be more exact. In his work the inspirited or meaningful human presence that we desire is always contained by and limited to the inert body we see; no transcendence is promised or possible and we are left to consider the "matte and somehow stupid" fact of the "absolute Particular" of a given face isolated in time. Nor could any description of the Realist project as a whole be more exact. Furthermore, in its utter mechanical subservience to the given circumstances or figures before it, photography is indeed the ideal Realist tool. What Baudelaire failed to recognize and what Barthes, no less the aesthete, so eloquently affirmed is that the poetry of the photograph resides in its transient or circumstantial quality. More than any other, the illusion of painting is one of timelessness. The photograph, in this regard, is without illusions. Barthes writes,

Painting can feign reality without having seen it. Discourse combines signs which have referents, of course, but these referents can be and most often are 'chimeras.' Contrary to these imitations, in Photography I can never deny that the thing has been there. . . . What I intentionalize in a photograph is neither Art nor Communication, it is Reference. . . . The name of Photography's noeme will therefore be: 'That has been' or again the Intractable.[13]

Here, then, not only Close's decision to replicate the photograph in painting but his specific choice of photographic genre as source material accentuates the tension between the enduring and endured image of painting and the static "present" of the camera. But if the family snapshot is valued precisely because it preserves an event that cannot be repeated or otherwise retrieved except as it is clouded and altered by memory—how difficult it is to remember a face we have known—the passport photograph, which records all the essential features of the human face, is an evidential instrument that presumes an unmistakable and abiding continuity of being.

Nevertheless, to sort through a stack of old passport photographs is to confront the basic fallacy of this assumption. For even if we have succeeded in each instance to compose our faces into the most agreeable and characteristic of expressions we know they will continue to age and change. The eternal sameness of the i.d. format only emphasizes the uncomfortable truth of this discovery. Yet, less cowed by the stern requirements of officialdom than hopeful of surviving as we conceived ourselves to be, we actively participate in this bureaucratic lie. To have such a photograph taken is not so much to document who we are, but how we want to be remembered. In fact, inasmuch as the object of our complicity is simply to be remembered at all, we may even be willing to sacrifice vanity for the sake of the illusion of permanence. To that end, any distinguishing feature, however unbecoming, is seized upon as evidence of our identity and confirmation of our constant selves. Thus "exposed," more than anything we resemble the men and women who, literally warts and all, confront us in the mortuary busts of the Late Roman Empire. What we project and then witness in a passport still is an image not lifelike but funereal. As Barthes writes, "Ultimately, what I am seeking in the photograph taken of me (the "intention" according to which I look at it) is Death: Death is the *eidos* of that Photograph."[14]

To speak then of the deadpan face we present to the camera is thus far more true than one would like to admit. It is the discomforting truth that Close's work forces us to acknowledge. In his paintings the "humanity" leached out of the image by a process of perpetual mechanical manipulation and reduction re-emerges, finally, not as a transcendent spiritual or aesthetic "aura" but as a tenuous, indeed absurd aspiration for what Eugene Ionesco has called "a temporary immortality." To be a subject of a Close portrait is to have the ephemeral nature of one's existence writ large. To look at his work is to experience vicariously, and perhaps only subliminally, one's own contingency. More than anything it is Close's unwelcome honesty in this respect that prompts the often negative response to his work. For, the coldness some people feel toward Close's paintings and the coldness of which Close has been accused is not just a consequence of his clinical technique or a matter of some affective debility in the artist. Although his paintings contain no overt emotion, the artist's exhaustive depictions are anything but a sign of the casual disregard for his subjects.

Close's Realism, in fact, precludes personal commentary or painterly caprice, and his strict adherence to that aesthetic is precisely what gives his work its claim to our attention. Rather what we feel, surrounded by Close's pantheon of the ordinary, is the chill of individual extinction. And if, as Baudelaire claimed, photography panders to the Narcissism of the common man, Close's unique synthesis of painting and photography turns the tables on the public, presenting it with a Narcissism astonishing in its candor and complete in its morbidity.

NOTES

1 For sections dealing with the history of photography the following two books served as my primary source or reference texts: Aaron Scharf, *Art and Photography* (New York: Penguin Books, 1983), and Van Deren Coke, *The Painter and the Photograph—from Delacroix to Warhol* (Albuquerque: University of New Mexico Press, 1964).

2 Charles Baudelaire, "The Salon of 1859—The Modern Public and Photography," *Baudelaire: Selected Writings on Art and Artists*, translated by P. E. Charvet (Cambridge: Cambridge University Press, 1972), p. 297.

3 Ibid., p. 296.

4 Ibid., p. 295.

5 Linda Nochlin, "The Realist Criminal and the Abstract Law II," *Art in America*, November—December 1973: 97—103.

6 Linda Nochlin, "The Realist Criminal and the Abstract Law," September—October 1973: 54—61.

7 Ibid., p. 54.

8 Barbaralee Diamonstein, "Chuck Close," in *Inside New York's Art World* (New York: Rizzoli International Publications, 1979), p. 70.

9 Walter Benjamin, "The Work of Art in the Age of Mechanical Reproduction," in *Illuminations*, edited and with an introduction by Hannah Arendt, translated by Harry Zohn (New York: Schocken Books, 1969), pp. 235—37.

10 Benjamin, "The Work of Art in the Age of Mechanical Reproduction," p. 220.

11 Diamonstein, "Chuck Close," p. 68.

12 Roland Barthes, *Camera Lucida: Reflections on Photography*, translated by Richard Howard (New York: Hill and Wang, 1981), p. 4.

13 Ibid., pp. 76—77.

14 Ibid., p. 15.

Installation of *Close Portraits* at The Walker Art Center, Minneapolis, 1980

EXPANDING THE LIMITS OF PORTRAITURE

LISA LYONS

THE only child of Leslie Durwood and Mildred Emma (Wagner) Close, Charles Thomas Close was born in Monroe, Washington, on July 5, 1940. Soon thereafter, the family moved to the nearby town of Everett and later to Tacoma.

Close speaks admiringly of his parents as creative, resourceful people. His father, who suffered a stroke and died when Close was eleven years old, was a jack-of-all-trades: a plumber, sheet-metal worker, and sometime inventor who made most of his son's toys—even trains and bicycles—from scratch. His mother was a gifted, classically trained pianist whose dreams of a concert career were crushed by the Depression. Her love of music never abated, however, and throughout Close's childhood, the house was filled with the piano students she took in to help support her family.

As a boy, Close was afflicted with a medical condition that affected his coordination and prevented him from participating in playground games. "I had Coke-bottle-bottom glasses and couldn't catch a ball to save my soul," he says. "If were playing a game and the kids started to run, I was soon left in the dust. So I determined that if I were going to have any friends at all, I would have to find ways to get people to come to me and stay put. I would have to learn to entertain the troops."[1]

With the help of his father, he built a backyard theater, where he presented elaborate puppet plays and magic shows. Soon the Close household became a gathering place for neighborhood kids. Offstage, the youthful impresario spent hours entertaining himself by drawing. "It was the first thing I was any good at, the first thing that really made me feel special," Close recalls. "And at the age of six when every other kid on the block wanted to be a policeman or a fireman, I wanted to be an artist." He was, in his own estimation, precocious, and long before most of his pals had mastered the intricacies of fingerpainting he was drawing in perspective. Recognizing their son's talent, his parents enrolled him in art classes taught by a neighbor. It was no ordinary atelier. "Looking back on it now," Close says, "I realize that it probably was a combination art school/whorehouse. The woman who taught the classes, I'm sure now, was a prostitute, and her johns were always knocking at the door. Of course, the nude models who posed for us were probably prostitutes as well."

With a few years of training at the bordello behind him, Close was on his way to becoming an accomplished Realist painter. But a visit to the Seattle Art Museum in 1953 changed his course. There he encountered some early "drip paintings" by Jackson Pollock.

Initially, Close was both outraged and confused by the audacious canvases with their tangled webs of paint, so unlike anything he had seen before. "But they hung with me, they haunted me," Close says, "and as soon as I got home, I began dripping and spattering aluminum paint and tar all over my own canvases. Up to that point, my hero had been Jan Vermeer. But overnight, I had become a junior Abstract Expressionist."

Although Close was a bright, creative child, he was not much of a student. Reading was sheer agony and he was hopeless at mathematics and spelling; but he found academic salvation in art. "I wasn't any good at the normal ways of proving my intelligence," Close explains, "so when I couldn't memorize names and dates, I would make things—like extra-credit, 10-foot-long murals of the Lewis and Clark Trail—to show the teacher that I cared about the material."

It was not until 1985 when he attended a lecture at his daughter's school that Close discovered the source of his scholastic difficulties. The subject was learning disabilities, and listening to the speaker, Close had the peculiar feeling that she was describing problems that had plagued him all his life: problems with reading, spelling, memorization, and ironically, considering that he is a portraitist, facial recognition. (Close claims that everyone he sees on the street looks vaguely familiar to him; passing acquaintances look as familiar as old friends.) "After attending the lecture, I took a couple of tests," he says. "The woman who tested me told me that I am the only person she knows with this particular form of dyslexia who isn't in prison. Apparently, similarly afflicted people often find it tough to fit into straight society, and so they turn to a life of crime. It's not that they're dumb. They're smart. Too smart to rob liquor stores but not too dumb to forge checks. Forgers! Pretty interesting when you consider the kind of painting I do....I guess you could say that I was predisposed to my profession."

Unfortunately, little was known about dyslexia in the 1950s, and the source of Close's academic problems went unrecognized by his junior high school advisor. Worse, she had little respect for his artistic talents. Viewing Close as a malingerer who would never amount to much of anything and was clearly not college material, she counseled him to consider taking up a trade. The impressionable teenager took her advice to heart and didn't sign up for any college preparatory classes. By the time he graduated from high school, however, he was determined to continue his education, and undaunted by his advisor's prognostications of failure, he enrolled in

The artist dressed as a magician, c. 1948

the junior college in his hometown with the intention of preparing for a career as a commercial artist. The curriculum included some studio arts courses, and as luck would have it, the school had an excellent painting faculty. "The administration was really proud of its artists," Close says. "In fact, it was the kind of place where the football team got new jerseys only if the art department didn't need supplies." Close quickly distinguished himself as a star pupil of the department and with the encouragement of his teachers, shifted his focus from the drafting table to the easel. His adolescent dreams of "working for Walt Disney or doing *Time* magazine covers" soon slipped away, supplanted by a new vision: he would be a painter.

In 1960, Close applied and was admitted to the University of Washington. There, as a member of that generation for whom Abstract Expressionism was the Academy, he produced works in the painterly style that had dominated American art for nearly twenty years. On the basis of these early efforts, he was invited to attend the Yale Summer School of Art and Music in 1961. The following year, upon receiving his bachelors degree, he left Seattle to begin graduate painting studies at Yale University.

"It was a time when it seemed as if the entire art world was plugged into New Haven," Close says. The Yale faculty included such luminaries of the contemporary painting scene as Jack Tworkov, Al Held, Alex Katz, William Bailey, and Philip Pearlstein. And the student roster read like a *Who's Who* of young American artists who were to come to prominence by the end of the decade. Brice Marden, Robert Mangold, Richard Serra, Nancy Graves, Rackstraw Downes, Janet Fish, Newton Harrison, Don Nice, and Jennifer Bartlett were all Close's classmates. The group was rambunctious. Close explains:

The administration considered us potential troublemakers—we had all been big ducks in our various little ponds—and segregated us from the rest of the students in a building all by ourselves. We painted all night long, had violent arguments, smashed furniture, threw loaded paint brushes at each other, and with all those egos hanging out, we sort of fought it out along the lines of whomever our particular gods were. Serra, for example, was interested for a time in Soutine, so he took out all the books in the library on him—and glued the pages together with paint. Then he moved on to Matisse. You could always tell who Richard was working on because you couldn't open any of the books. But he wasn't alone. We all unabashedly copied and borrowed from other artists. It wasn't a matter of postmodern appropriation. We were those artists. I was de Kooning. Serra was Hofmann. Rackstraw was Al Held. Brice Marden was probably the only person

who did any kind of work that resembled his mature work. Everyone else was hopelessly lost in a very interesting way.

Not only were they lost, but they were rooted in the past—so much so that Robert Rauschenberg, who lectured at Yale in the early 1960s, declared that "the place reeked of Matisse." That is not to say that the students were unaware of or disinterested in contemporary art. In fact, they frequently visited the New York galleries, and Close remembers being particularly impressed with the work of the Pop artists, especially Roy Lichtenstein, Andy Warhol, and James Rosenquist. But as a dedicated abstractionist, he was somewhat suspicious of this new form of Realism. And in any case, he viewed his plodding journey through the history of art and his apprenticeship to older masters as crucial to his artistic development. Only by completely digesting earlier styles, he reasoned, could he then purge all references to those styles from his own painting.

Not a bad theory. But the purge was neither thorough nor immediately apparent, for throughout graduate school Close produced richly hued biomorphic abstractions that owed a large debt to de Kooning's "pink angel" paintings. On the basis of these, he graduated with honors from Yale and received a Fulbright Fellowship to study in Vienna at the Akademie der Bildenden Kunste in 1964.

There he paid daily visits to the Kunsthistorisches Museum. He spent hours studying its extraordinary collection which ranges from Greek and Roman antiquities to the Old Masters. But he was especially attracted to the museum's Northern Renaissance and seventeenth-century Dutch paintings and remembers lingering over his longtime hero Jan Vermeer's masterpiece, *The Artist in the Studio*. To this day, Close can describe its complex composition in intimate, centimeter-by-centimeter detail. He also spent considerable time traveling to other cities and digesting what he calls the "gemüstesalat" of European art history. "It was both wonderful and numbing seeing all that art," Close recalls. "I found it nearly impossible to paint. I came to feel the incredible weight of the historical baggage that a European painter must carry with him every time he approaches the canvas. And I developed a real appreciation for the freedom that American artists have by virtue of the relative lack of indigenous painting traditions and conventions in the U.S."

Toward the middle of his European sojourn, Close joined his Yale classmate and fellow Fulbright recipient, Kent Floeter, on the Costa Brava in Spain. One night conversation turned to their future plans. Envisioning themselves returning home by ship to New York and

The artist in his studio at Yale University, c. 1964

then standing on the pier with all their possessions and no place to go, they panicked. By morning they had found the solution to their problem: they would apply for teaching positions. A few months later Floeter landed a job as chairman of the art department at Ithaca College, and Close shipped off to the University of Massachusetts in Amherst.

Close describes his two years on the Amherst faculty as a difficult period, personally and professionally: "The first year I was a painter who also taught. By the second year, I had made the incredible transition to a teacher who also painted. I drank a lot, got involved in antiwar politics and almost stopped painting altogether." When he did work, he faced the dilemma of enjoying making art, but not liking what he made. "I had a good hand. I was very facile, but I lacked discipline," Close admits. "Even though I had all the options in the world open to me, every time I set brush to canvas, I made the same old shapes. I kept using the same half-dozen color combinations."

Eventually he became so disturbed by his increasingly predictable work habits that he abandoned the familiar turf of open-ended abstraction for an area he knew very little about: figuration. "In the past, I've probably made it sound like a clear, rational choice, but there was a kind of desperation in my decision to stop painting abstractions," Close said recently. "I needed to find a way of working that would help me stabilize my life. I wanted to find something specific to do, something with its own set of rights and wrongs." Having been thwarted in his attempts to invent new forms and subjects, Close began to use found imagery as the point of departure for his work. Magazine photographs, wedding pictures, even record-album covers became the basis for mixed-media constructions in which he explored relationships between reality and illusion, and more specifically, between the human figure and its painted depiction. Most of these works were shallow reliefs in which figures were painted in skewed perspective on transparent Plexiglas sheets. Three-dimensional elements—lifelike hands fashioned of vacuum-formed plastic and trompe l'oeil cardboard walls—projected from either side of the relief surface, creating a sense of palpable space both in front of and behind the picture plane.

Close found the results of this foray into figuration inconclusive, and he eventually destroyed the constructions. The use of photographs still held promise, however, for he recognized that camera images might provide precise models against which he could measure his accomplishments objectively. To control his results further,

he decided to make his own photographs and to limit his activities to recording only that information contained within the prints. And by working in extremely large scale, he reasoned, he could make that information not only accessible but unavoidable.

Close began making real progress toward his mature style in 1966 when he shot some black-and-white photographs of a young woman who was employed as a secretary at the University of Massachusetts. He used these as a basis for what was intended to be a reclining nude of gigantic proportions painting in "living color." Only a small portion of the mammoth odalisque was complete when Close realized that there were serious flaws in his approach. In trying to paint the nude's flesh tones from a black-and-white photograph he was forced to invent color. Furthermore, by applying opaque pigments with traditional brush techniques, he failed to achieve the precise effect he was after. Reluctantly, he abandoned the canvas.

Close's idealistic vision of "teaching in the boondocks, getting a nice, comfortable salary and being an artist" had evaporated by the fall of 1967, and he moved to New York with his girlfriend, Leslie Rose. The couple, who married later that year, set up a studio on Greene Street in the area that would become SoHo. In those days there were no galleries, no wine bars, no trendy boutiques—none of the accoutrements of gentrified urban chic for which the neighborhood is now renowned. "There were probably about a dozen artists living between Canal and Houston," Close recollects. "At night when we'd walk down the street, we'd see a light on only every four or five blocks. And all day Sunday you could lie down in the middle of Greene Street and a car would never come by." The Closes' loft had no heat or hot water, but the rent was cheap and the place was spacious. Leslie was studying sculpture at Hunter College, and Chuck was earning enough money to support the two of them by teaching two days a week at the School of Visual Arts. Many nights were spent debating the burning art issues of the day with friends at Max's Kansas City on Park Avenue or Remington's, a bar in the old Broadway Central Hotel, which has long since met the wrecking ball. And several afternoons Close joined a crew that included the composers Philip Glass and Steve Reich, the writer Rudy Wurlitzer, and the filmmakers Bob Fiore and Michael Snow, whom Richard Serra corralled to assemble his massive lead sculptures. "It was an exciting time in our lives," Close says. "There was a nice sense of a community of younger artists evolving and an extraordinary exchange of ideas."

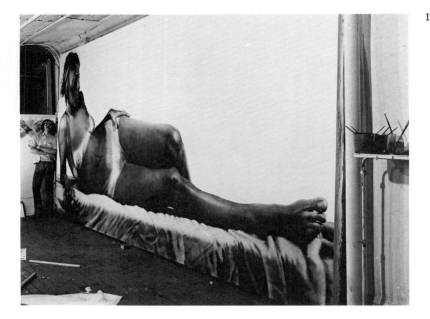

Meanwhile, back at his studio, Close was making a second all-out attempt at working from the photographs of the Massachusetts *maja*. This time he limited his palette to black and white. He nailed a 22-foot-long canvas to the wall and began to experiment. First he painted the figure's right foot, then he shifted to the other end of the canvas to work on her head. By the time he had traversed the surface several weeks later, it had become a testing ground for many systems of getting paint on—and off—the canvas. His battery of tools included brushes, sponges, rags, spray guns, razor blades, even a pencil eraser stuck into the end of an electric drill.

Though the monumental painting was an effective learning device, the result was "an erratic anthology of styles and techniques . . . too inconsistent and obviously too confused to be shown."[2] Aside from its uneven technical qualities, Close disliked other aspects of the work. In making the painting, he had tried to treat every part of the figure with equal importance. "It was connected to the notion of all-overness that came out of Jackson Pollock," Close says. "I had the belief that the essential American image at that point, whether it was Pollock or Stella, had a consistent surface . . . and that every piece was essentially the same. I wanted to approach the nude with that same kind of lack of hierarchy . . . in a deadpan, dumb kind of way." But in fact certain areas of the painting were more interesting than others. As Close notes with some amusement, friends invited to view the canvas tended to congregate in front of two "hot spots"—the nude's crotch and her pendulous breasts. There was another problem: although the painting was 22 feet long, Close felt that the scale of the nude was still too small to convey the kind and degree of information he was after.

One afternoon, while photographing this unresolved painting, Close found that he had some extra film in the studio. As he stood there contemplating his next shot, his attention shifted from the great earth mother on the wall to himself. "I wanted to get away from 'hot' subject matter and I wanted bigger scale," Close says, "so I decided to focus on some other part of the body. The head seemed an obvious choice." Alone in the studio, he positioned himself squarely in front of the camera and released the shutter.

The result was a head-and-shoulders, passport-style shot showing Close as the quintessential angry young man of the 1960s with a cigarette drooping from his lips. ("I guess I had seen too many James Dean movies," he says.) Because he had photographed himself slightly from below and had misjudged the focal length of the camera lens, certain areas of the image were out of focus. These mis-

takes intrigued him because he felt that "they did interesting spatial things to the image . . . they added another kind of information to deal with, something to paint. That range of focus also allowed for a potentially more abstract reading of the image."

Stretching and gessoing a 9 x 7-foot canvas with proportions approximating those of the photograph, Close set to work on a self-portrait. In translating the photograph into a monumental painting, Close used the technique devised by Renaissance masters and adapted by contemporary billboard painters. He overlaid the photograph with a grid, then square by square transferred the image in pencil to the white canvas. Then using an airbrush loaded with a thin mixture of black acrylic paint and water, he began to spray in the eyes—the area with the sharpest focus. Working from top to bottom, he then roughed in the rest of the image with a fine spray of paint, and slowly added pigment to build up the darker tones. Some highlights were defined by white paint, but the pigment tended to build up and become chalky and opaque. Consequently, most of the minute shiny details were created by removing paint and revealing the underlying layer of gesso. For example, the illusion of light glancing off the hairs of his beard was achieved by scratching into the paint with a razor blade; an electric eraser produced the reflections of the floodlamps in the lenses of his glasses.

Close worked nearly four months on the self-portrait, and although it was an arduous process he found the experience liberating. Ironically, by limiting himself to recording only that information contained within the photograph, he found he was actually making shapes and patterns that were totally new, unlike any he had invented as an abstractionist. Equally important, he had finally found genuine criteria against which he could judge his paintings. A shape not in the photograph was wrong, but an accurately transcribed detail was right.

With the self-portrait, Close established the basic elements of his style: large scale, anonymous surface, formula composition, and photographic veracity. He refined and explored these characteristics in a series of enormous black-and-white portrait heads that occupied him until April 1970.

For these, Close decided to use only friends as subjects. "Quite honestly," Close says, "if you're going to spend several months painting a face, it makes the job easier and infinitely more important if it belongs to someone you care about." Then as now, he had no interest in making Pop icons à la Andy Warhol's superstar pictures or in painting commissioned portraits of college presidents and

politicians, though many such opportunities have come his way. The relative anonymity of his subjects, he once said, forces viewers to confront his works as "paintings first and portraits second." Ironically, however, as Thomas Hess observed, the subjects of Close's early works have since assumed "the air of an existential pantheon, a SoHo apotheosis . . . superstars all in the exploding inevitable history of art."[3] Among his once-anonymous subjects are such now well-known artists as Richard Serra, Nancy Graves, and Joe Zucker, composer Philip Glass, and opera designer Bob Israel.

The seven portraits that Close produced between 1968 and 1970 were all created through the same methodical process of transferring mosaics of visual information from the photograph onto a 9 x 7-foot gessoed canvas. The resulting images are remote documentations of faces as seen through a camera viewfinder. Indeed, those who encounter a Close portrait for the first time often mistake the painting for a colossal, amazingly detailed photograph. At a distance the viewer is aware only of the head itself, a convincingly modeled form. Moving in for a closer look, all perception of the Brobdingnagian image begins to dissipate. Now the viewer is confronted by the minutiae of human physiognomy as recorded by the camera and translated by the painter. The surface of the face becomes a vast landscape where pores are craters, wrinkles are ravines. Closer still, all illusion of depth and volume gives way to an awareness of the canvas surface, a white plane energized by amorphous black-and-white painted shapes.

In each portrait, the tip of the nose is a bit fuzzy, as are the ears. Only the eyes and parts of the cheeks are critically defined. Consequently, a vivid sensation of depth and volume is established. In *Phil*, 1969, for example, the eyes appear to be on the same level as the picture plane; the nose and an unruly shock of hair hover out in front; and the ears and shoulders are set well back in space. In Close's words, the overall impression is of "sharp focus data within a sandwich of blur."

Close's gargantuan amplification and faithful interpretation of the camera's vision are disorienting. No matter how long and hard we look at the paintings, no matter where we choose to stand, the focus cannot be resolved. His treatment of scale is equally complex. Large scale has been hallmark of American painting ever since the Abstract Expressionists abandoned the easel to create mural-size works, and Close's portraits are within this tradition. But as John Roy, the subject of Close's 1971–72 portrait, *John*, observed, when the Abstract Expressionists' paintings became larger, so did the

size and sweep of their brushwork. As a result, the scale—the relationships of part to whole—actually remained the same. Close, by contrast, makes works of extremely large size without increasing the size of his marks.[4] Thus, except at a distance, it is virtually impossible to read the heads as unitary images. Moving in for a closer look, we inevitably fall under the spell of the astonishing wealth of detail recorded on the canvas. Confronting *Frank*, 1969, for instance, we can get lost in the forest of his beard and the warped reflections of a bank of windows in his glasses.

Occasionally, even Close is seduced by his own illusionism. He recalls a particularly disturbing situation while working on the portrait of Bob Israel:

I had taken a break and was walking back into the studio. Looking at the painting, I noticed that a highlight in one of the eyes was too bright. And I said, 'Damn it, now I'm going to have to take his glasses off to fix it.' But when I realized what I had said, I pivoted on my heel and walked out leaving the lights on, the compressor on and the airbrushes full of paint. When you start believing in your own illusion, you're in serious trouble.

But Close rarely loses his seemingly bloodless objectivity towards his work. His method of painting—one which requires discipline and self-abnegation—was chosen for practical reasons. It allows him to work independent of daily mood and to maintain stylistic consistency over the many months required to produce each large painting. "My work habits are a reaction to my own nature. My nature is that I am nervous, sloppy, lazy," Close admits. "If I lived in California, I'd say, 'Hey, that's the way I am,' and I would make a nervous, sloppy, quick painting that was an attempt to 'go with it.' So I've constructed a situation in which I can't behave in a lazy way, I can't behave in a sloppy way, and I have to somehow deal with my nervousness." He tends to describe his method of composition in purely formal terms: "I have a system for how the head is going to fit into the rectangle. The head is going to be so big, it is going to come so close to the top edge, and it is going to be centered left and right." He has also said that in making a painting, he is often "not conscious of making a nose or an eye, but only of distributing pigment on a flat surface."

His ability to maintain this remote, intellectualized stance and the coolness of his style have led many observers to believe that Close lacks any interest in his subjects as human beings. Witness the critic Robert Hughes: "Above all there is no character analysis. . . . About Close's sitters one learns nothing—except that they

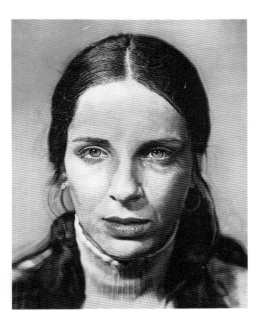

have more pores than the travertine of the Coliseum. One's curiosity about who they may be is stifled by Close's relentless forensic approach. The images verify without interpreting."[5] This reading has surely been bolstered by the fact that, unlike traditional portrait painters, Close has no need of live models. As Martin Friedman, director of Walker Art Center, Minneapolis, has pointed out, once Close has a usable photograph in hand, the model can go his own way. Thus, his paintings are portraits of *photographs* of his subjects—never of the subjects themselves.[6] Close is convinced, however, that a photograph made in a fraction of a second captures some special truth about a person. An objective, photographic portrayal of a face as a "roadmap of human experience," he believes, may ultimately afford more insight into a subject's personality than a traditional portrait painter will reveal through the contact of lengthy sittings:

Live models change. They gain weight, they lose weight; one day they're happy, the next day they're sad; one day they're awake, the next day they're tired. All these things happen, and as a result, the painting becomes the mean average of all these experiences. The thing I like about a photograph is that it represents a frozen, poemlike moment in time. It remains constant, and the painting, however long it takes to make, is always about that quintessential moment.

Reliving that moment can be an unsettling experience for those select few who allow Close to, as he says, "steal their faces." In fact, a subject's initial confrontation with his vastly magnified mug can be downright traumatic. Close himself admits to being disturbed by his own billboard-scale surrogate: "The self-portrait became a magnification of my flaws . . . my lima bean nostrils, my ears, my balding head. Things that I didn't like about myself, the way I looked, became enlarged to such an extent that they were impossible to ignore. . . . I couldn't deal with the fact that it was me. I referred to the painting as *him*."

Leslie Close was eager to pose for her husband and admits that she "pestered Chuck from the day he started painting, 'do me, do me, do me.' I used to tease him that some historian would make a very big point of the fact that he had never painted his wife."[7] In 1972 she got her wish, and though she likes the work, Close says, "she finds it difficult to confront the image. She can't even go near it." Mark Greenwold, whose broad, bespectacled face has been the subject of several Close works since 1978, had a somewhat more positive reaction to his painted portrayals: "I like the paintings. . . . I don't find them monstrous or shocking. But one subtle, slightly

frightening thing happened, and I have no idea whether or not it's connected with Chuck's painting me. Shortly after he started the series of works based on my image, I grew a beard and haven't shaved it off since."[8] Mark is not alone. In fact, virtually all of Close's subjects have made changes in their appearances after having seen their paintings. New glasses and new hairstyles are common responses. The only person not to have done that is Joe Zucker. Close explains:

Joe Zucker is one of the most atypical people I've ever met. And typically his solution was atypical. When I went to pick him up to photograph him, I didn't recognize him. He has curly, blond, bushy hair—but he had bought a jar of vaseline, greased his hair down, borrowed someone else's white shirt and tie, someone else's glasses and he looked like a used-car salesman. He understood that all he had to do was provide me with the evidence that someone like that existed for one-hundredth of a second. It didn't necessarily have to be him, he didn't have to identify with it. After the photo session he went home and washed the grease out of his hair and went back to life as usual.

Zucker's ploy underscores not only the photographic nature but also the artificiality of Close's painting. For all their specificity, his portraits are also abstract images, and the formal base underlying their realistic facades is always apparent. A case could be made, in fact, for considering his early canvases as field paintings, for they are symmetrical compositions whose surfaces contain no evidence of the artist's "handwriting." And because Close's paintings are generated by intricate grid systems, they can be compared to the work of such artists as Donald Judd and Sol LeWitt. But Close's reductivist methods result in what he calls "maximal" compositions, essentially opposite in style and spirit to the spare works of the Minimalists. The paradoxical character of Close's paintings—a delicate balance of description and abstraction, idea and image, process and product—is their strength.

In 1969 Close was invited by Klaus Kertess to join the Bykert Gallery and that same year his work was included in the Whitney Museum of American Art's annual exhibition of contemporary American art. He was beginning to achieve critical recognition, he landed a teaching job at New York University and with the sale of several paintings, he and Leslie were able to move from their Greene Street studio into a new loft on Prince Street in the spring of 1970. All in all, things were going well for Close, but he felt that he had reached an impasse in his work. Having completed eight black-and-white

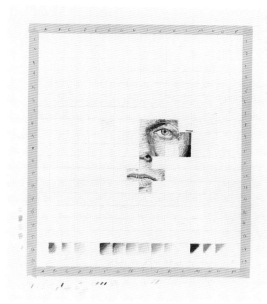

portrait heads, he had refined his technique to a virtually unsurpassable degree. Feeling that "there were no surprises in the studio anymore," he began to consider his options:

The first thing that occurred to me was to change the subject matter, but I wasn't tired with the image, only with the process, with not having anything new to think about in the studio. I wanted a real change, one that would affect the way I thought, the tools I used . . . and that's when I decided to get color back into my paintings.

Close had purged color from his work in 1967 because he had "become too dependent on certain learned color relationships." To avoid slipping back into old habits, he sought a way of producing color without actually inventing it, that is, without mixing pigments on a palette. "When you mix color on a palette," Close explains, "you're mixing it out of context and you hope it's right. If it's not the right green, you can still say, 'Well, it's not the right green, but it's close enough' or 'It's not the right green, but I like it anyway.' So I looked for a way of working where all the paint would physically mix on the canvas, *in situ* where I could see what I was doing."

He invited several friends to the studio for photo sessions and from the numerous sheets of color film he shot, he selected a transparency of Kent Floeter. Then he began to experiment with a technique of painting similar to the photomechanical process by which color reproductions are printed. A photographic lab provided him with three continuous-tone separations of the transparency: one magenta (red), one cyan (blue), one yellow. Five dye-transfer prints were made from these in sequence: magenta; cyan; magenta plus cyan; yellow; and magenta plus cyan plus yellow. Close used these as working drawings for two color pencil studies and a watercolor produced during the summer of 1970. The most complex of these is the watercolor version, a mosaiclike composition that reproduces gridded fragments of Kent's face. A color key at the bottom of the sheet reveals Close's technique of overlaying the three hues in sequence to produce full color. Portions of the face, the nose and lips for example, were painted only in magenta; with the addition of cyan the left eye was taken a step further to the purple stage. Only the right eye and a bit of cheek received the final yellow overlay to create full color.

Pleased with the results of his experiments, Close selected acrylic paints that matched the photographic dyes in hue and intensity and set to work on a 9 x 7-foot gessoed canvas. Using the gridded dye-transfer prints as his guides, he proceeded to paint three one-color paintings on top of each other. Staying within boundaries defined by wrinkles, scars, shadows, or edges, he painted small areas of the face, and in each he laid down the red pigment first, then worked over the area with blue and finally with yellow. The background was reproduced in this precise manner, even though it happens to be a fairly uniform shade of gray.

The complexity of this technique cannot be underestimated. Most difficult of all, Close says, was determining just how much of each color should be applied to the surface. In *Kent* and two subsequent paintings, portrayals of his father-in-law Nat Rose and the artist Susan Zucker, Close wore tinted cellophane filters over his glasses as he worked. The filters cancelled out the underlying hues and allowed him to see only the color he was spraying out of the airbrush. By the time he began the portrait of the painter John Roy, in 1971, however, Close had mastered the technique sufficiently to discard the filters and to judge intuitively the correct amount of density of each hue to be applied.

Each of these continuous-tone paintings required fourteen months of painstaking labor, as Close wryly comments:

Sometimes I laugh because making a painting is such a long and involved process. I'll spend three weeks gessoing and wet-sanding a canvas—ten to twelve coats—getting it all smooth and getting it perfect and it reminds me of those apartment signs you see on the highway, 'If you lived here you'd be home now.' If I were Robert Ryman, I'd be done. And then I spend another two weeks getting a fine pencil grid on the canvas, and if I were Agnes Martin, I'd be done. And then my work has just begun. I've got ten more months of work to do.

Does Close find this lengthy process boring? "I have to admit that sometimes I do," he says, then quickly adds that earlier as an abstract painter, "I painted with my raw nerve endings dangling and I painted with my gut and I was a nervous wreck. I wasn't bored a lot, but I didn't paint much either and most important, I didn't like what I made." Today Close keeps regular studio hours, arriving there by 8:30 A.M. and working until about 4:00 P.M. "Then the whistle blows and I go home," he says. Painting has become a much less emotional enterprise, "one with fewer of the highs I used to have in the studio, but I also don't have the tremendous lows that would come when the whole painting would fall apart in front of my eyes."

Close derives a great deal of pleasure from watching an image unfold. "It is rather like magic," he says. "When I get to the last color, yellow, you can't see the pigment come out of the airbrush—it's like waving a magic wand in front of the picture, and the purple

becomes brown. It's really quite wonderful." Nonetheless, he finds the work extremely demanding—physically and psychologically. To make maneuvering over the expansive canvas surfaces easier, he devised an ingenious "mobile studio" consisting of a cutaway booth on the steel prongs of a Big Joe forklift. Sitting in its chair, he can raise or lower himself and reach any spot of the canvas simply by pulling on a rope. Propped on an easel to his left are the gridded photographs he refers to as he paints; a shelf on the right carries a telephone and two other important pieces of equipment: a television and a radio/cassette deck. The background noise they provide helps him to maintain that subtle degree of detachment he needs from the tedious activity of building an image, part by part, with machinelike precision. In the past, Close listened to (but did not watch) television almost constantly while working, becoming in the process a connoisseur of morning game shows and afternoon soap operas. Their slow-paced soundtracks are "of such a mundane nature that you don't really get engaged," he once said. "It's like having a dumb friend in the room. It just chatters away and you don't have to respond to it." These days, Close is hooked on news programs. On a marathon painting day, when the heat is on to complete a work, he might "catch the *Today Show*, then tune to another channel for the prenoon news, then get the noon news on another, then get the afternoon news on another, and then get the five o'clock news, the local news at six o'clock, the national news at seven o'clock and then the MacNeil/Lehrer Newshour." Other days he listens to "radio shrinks" or classical music. He usually finds the insistent beat of rock music too compelling, except when he is on the home stretch of a large-scale painting. Then he cranks up the volume and plays Aretha Franklin's *Greatest Hits* tape, "as a way of celebrating."

Close's process of building an image from just three hues occasionally results in garish tonalities recalling the "larger than life" color of slick magazine illustrations and Technicolor movies. *Linda*, 1975–76 and *Mark*, 1978, for example, seem bathed in an intense red light. "It's not that Linda and Mark are red in real life," Close says, "but that the red separations I used for these images contained the greatest amount of information about the subjects' faces. So I used a relatively larger proportion of red than either blue or yellow pigment to make the paintings."

Less aggressive, but no less compelling than these florid images, is Close's 1971–72 portrait, *John*. Posed frontally in typical Close mug-shot fashion, the figure looks out from behind wire-rimmed glasses with slightly squinting eyes. A shock of hair falls across his brow and his upper lip and chin are obscured by a full mustache and beard. Rendered with clarity at the front, his tangled facial hairs merge into a soft hazy mass at either side as they meet his shirt collar. His jacket is a sea of swirling color.

In its vast scale, formal pose, and fixed, hypnotic stare, this hieratic visage bears comparison with such Late Roman portraits as the fourth-century A.D. colossal head of Constantine. Like that impassive being, which has been alternately interpreted as an icon of spiritual determination or uncertainty, John seems somehow remote from the viewer's space.[9] His gaze never really meets our own. Rather, his eyes are directed slightly down and to his right, focused, one supposes, on the single eye of the camera. As a result, the image is difficult to penetrate. This disquieting sensation is heightened by the amorphous background of the painting. When Close's monochromatic paintings are installed on white walls, as he prefers, their uninflected grounds seem to merge with the hanging surface. Consequently, the heads appear to advance as volumetric forms. But the atmospheric gray field behind John's head contrasts with the white wall, making the head appear flatter and somewhat recessed, as if seen through a window. This illusion of physical distance increases the psychological distance between spectator and image. Confronting John, then, we are faced with a paradox. We are at once drawn into the work, seduced by Close's detailed description of the model, and yet separated from it.

Since 1971 Close has experimented with watercolor, a medium that requires considerable facility and leaves little margin for error. But Close has mastered this difficult medium, producing a series of portraits roughly half the scale of his acrylic paintings that are imbued with an appealing immediacy and freshness. In a tour de force grisaille self-portrait, the artist's glasses cast distracting shadows and his short beard, with its kinky hairs bristling this way and that, is an agitated thicket of energy. The color portrait of Leslie Close, by contrast, is serene and placid, a contemporary madonna whose translucent skin has an ethereal glow. Close allows that its success is due in part to the peculiar qualities of watercolors, which allow him to achieve greater control of value, hue, and intensity than is possible with acrylics. Whereas the plastic paint tends to build up, leaving a film of the last color applied to the surface, transparent watercolors mix more completely and soak into the paper. As a result, the image appears to be part of the surface, as in a stained, color-field painting. Moreover, because the pigment is

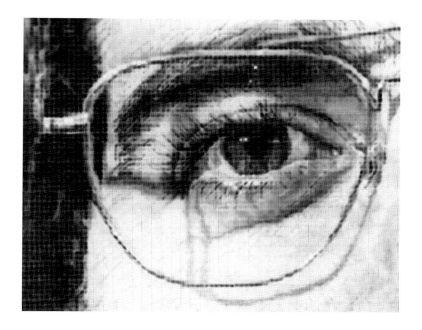

ground so finely and held in a thin watery suspension, light easily passes through the paint and is reflected by the white ground.

Discussing his paintings, Close frequently makes references to architecture. He compares the process of making a continuous tone painting to "building a wall, brick by brick." But the painstaking labor involved in creating their seamless surfaces is invisible. There is no evidence of the grid system that generates them. In several works produced since the early 1970s, however, Close has revealed his modular technique.

In 1972 Close was approached by Bob Feldman, owner of Parasol Press, to produce a print in collaboration with Kathan Brown at San Francisco's Crown Point Press. He was hesitant to accept the invitation because, as he explains, "I've always disliked certain aspects of print shops—the high dependency on machinery and technology, and the fact that printers known something that you don't know. You don't know what's possible; you don't even know the right questions to ask. So you make some kind of little drawing and you hand it over to them and at the end of the process something comes out and it usually looks more like a product of the print shop than a product of the artist."

But Feldman was persistent, and Close ultimately agreed to make a print, choosing as his subject the same photograph that had been the basis of his 1970 painting *Keith*. To assure his active participation in the printing process, Close elected to work in mezzotint. Prized by nineteenth-century artists for its extraordinary tonal range, the medium had fallen into disuse after the development of photoengraving. "I figured that since nobody knew how to make a mezzotint, we were all going to be in the soup together," Close recalled. "I would learn, the printers would learn, and the work would be a real collaboration."

Having painted for so long on canvas taller than himself, Close must have felt cramped working on a plate that measured 44½ x 35 inches. Even so, the plate was larger than any etching press had ever handled, and in typical Close fashion, the print's creation was a labor-intensive enterprise. The traditional mezzotint process begins with a completely black plate, which has been uniformly roughened with a tool known as a rocker to produce a nap that holds the ink. Light tones are achieved by selectively smoothing down the nap. To achieve a richer, denser surface than would have been possible with hand tools, Close first had the plate photographically etched. Then he spent six weeks dividing the plate into dozens of

one-inch-square units and manually burnishing the burrs of each area to create the image.[10] The finished print closely resembles the 1970 painting of Keith, particularly in its concentration on the details of flesh. What differentiates it is the evidence of its creation: a grid, scratched into the plate, fades from view in the velvety black expanse of Keith's turtleneck sweater and jacket but is clearly visible across his face. There the individual squares are set off by tonal differences caused in part by the pulling of proofs of state, a process that eroded the copperplate. This technical glitch would be unacceptable to most print purists, but Close was pleased with its effect on the image. The grid's visibility, he feels, clarifies his analytical attitude toward Realism. Unlike the typical graphic work that simply supplements an artist's production ("a 'souvenir' with an artist's signature," as Close put it), the mezzotint is a fully independent work that contributes to a deeper understanding of his techniques and intentions.

Once Close had allowed the grid to surface in the mezzotint, it was there to stay. In a series of works begun in 1973, which the artist terms "dot drawings," it became an ever-more insistent presence.

The dot drawings are records of Close's long-stated ambition to imbue every square inch of canvas with equal importance. He fell short of doing this in the paintings, he says, because in making them "it was necessary to behave one way when you make the hair, another way when you make the background and another way when you make the skin." Unlike the continuous tone works, however, there is no range in the size and shape of the marks used to depict the facial features in the drawings; there are no graphic symbols for hair, nose, eyes, or lips. Rather realism is reduced to a code, a simple system of identical marks, repeated over and over again. The images are composed of tiny, equal-size dots set into taut grids ranging from eleven squares horizontally in the minuscule *Robert I/154*, 1974, to over 200 in the 9 x 7-foot *Robert/104,072*, 1973–74.

Like his paintings, the drawings were executed with an airbrush. In these works, however, Close made no use of the instrument's capacity for blending. Modeling was achieved, instead, by varying pigment densities: shadows are described by dots that were hit several times with the airbrush, highlights by those that received a smaller dose of ink.

As Robert Hughes has observed, if Close's large-scale paintings are about the upper limits of perception—the point at which a face almost dissolves in a welter of visual data—then the dot drawings

are about the lower limits. How little information do you need to recognize a face? How generalized can it be before the specific relationship of features falls apart? And which features are the first to disappear?[11] Close systematically explored these questions in a series of four drawings based on a single photograph of Bob Israel. The sizes of the paper and of the dots remain constant throughout the series, as the number of dots and grid squares quadruples from one drawing to the next. As a result, the size and resolution of the images progressively increase. The image in *Bob I/154*, for example, is an indistinct smudge no bigger than a postage stamp at the center of a white field; the image in *Bob IV/9,856*, by contrast, is a clearly legible face covering most of the sheet.

A variety of philosophical and formal associations relates Close's dot drawings to other phenomena in contemporary art. The idea of building an image from repeatable units has its origins in the concerns of several artists whose work of the 1960s spans a broad stylistic spectrum. Frank Stella's stripe paintings and Andy Warhol's repetitive soup cans are examples. As Kim Levin has noted, the elaborate grid systems and titles of Close's drawings which refer to the number of dots in an image parallel the concerns of the minimal artist Sol LeWitt.[12] One thinks, too, of the work of Close's contemporary, Jennifer Bartlett. Like her compositions of painted dots set into fastidiously defined grids, Close's drawings suggest a fusion of late nineteenth-century Pointillism and mid-1960s Minimalism.

Other relationships are detectable. Drawings that exist in series of four, with their increases in the size of the central rectangle and concomitant shrinking of the framing edge, seem to parody Josef Albers's *Homage to the Square* series. But Close, who studied at Yale among Albers's disciples, denies being influenced by Albers, "unless it's unconsciously. It was pretty hard to take that stuff seriously by the time it had been passed on," he says.[13] Close, however, *does* admire the paintings of Ad Reinhardt in which barely perceptible cruciforms float within black matrices. A similar use of closely related hues characterizes dot drawings such as *Keith*, 1973, a black image on a black field. Only after lengthy concentration does the viewer comprehend the face.

By the mid-1970s Close was firmly established as a major talent of his generation. His work had been shown in more than sixty exhibitions at museums and galleries throughout the United States, Europe, and Japan. Virtually every one of his paintings, drawings,

and prints had been acquired for important public and private collections. In 1977, following the demise of the Bykert Gallery, Close was invited by Arnold Glimcher to join the prestigious Pace Gallery, where he continues to show.

Today, nearly twenty years since his work first appeared on the scene, Close continues to be best known for his monumental acrylic portraits, though these constitute only a small portion of his overall production. In fact, since 1975 his energies have been largely devoted to works in other media. He has, for example, produced a large body of smaller works on paper which have allowed him, as he says, to "program change" into his approach at a faster rate than was previously possible. In sometimes subtle, but nonetheless important ways, these works constitute a radical departure from the reductivist techniques that characterize his earlier creations.

In the black-and-white compositions that Close has produced since the mid-1970s, he has considerably enriched his formal vocabulary of marks and techniques. The images in a pair of self-portrait prints dating from 1977 and 1978, for example, were built from diagonal lines, recalling the hatchmarks of old master etchings. Superficially, these images, with their stepped contours, look as though they might have been generated by a computer, but closer examination reveals the irregularities of the thousands of tiny lines. Subtle as they may be, they are indications of the artist's hand.

This tension between the mechanical and manual elements of his style is intensified in a series of works, begun in 1978, that literally bear his mark: the fingerprint drawings. Although an irrefutable sign of personal identity, the fingerprint for Close is just another easily repeated abstract shape. Inking his finger, he makes numerous impressions on the paper surface and changes their tonality by varying the pressure of his hand. In a 1978 drawing of Robert, he stamped the eccentric oval, unit by unit, into a grid. Canted diagonally and sometimes bleeding across the lines, the fingerprints all but obliterate the penciled lattice. In two other drawings of Robert, Close used an acetate mask to produce discrete marks that look like grouted tiles.

In the fingerprint pieces Close has produced since 1980, among them an 8 x 6-foot image of Phil, he has completely abandoned the grid, applying his marks randomly across the surface at various angles. Whether the drawing was made quickly or not, it has been noted, the image looks "fast and fresh, managing to give the simultaneous impression of great freedom and superb control."[14] By

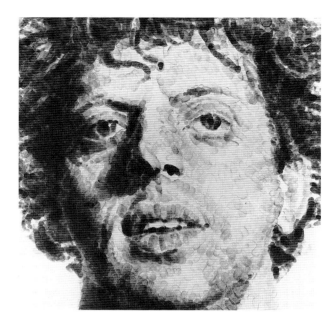

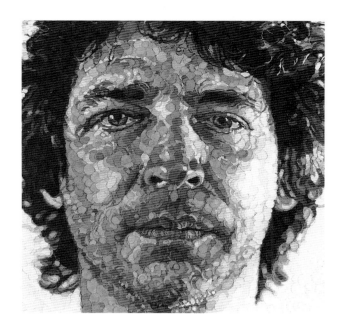

Left: **LARGE PHIL FINGERPRINT/RANDOM, 1979**
Right: **JUD, 1982**

randomly applying the fingerprint, Close has given the surface a richness absent from his earlier images of Phil. The face is convincingly modeled, but the baroque whorl patterns swarming over its surface remind us that this portrait is a composition of abstract marks on a flat surface.

In a discussion about these works, Close pointed to a book illustration of a tantric sri yantra—a diagram meant to stimulate meditation.[15] According to the caption, the diagram had lost its power and was reactivated by gurus who pressed red ink impressions of their thumbs onto its surface. It is easy to see why Close likes the picture; he, too, has reactivated his images by similar means.

In 1981 Close was approached by Joseph Wilfer, a printer and papermaker, who was eager to collaborate with him on a project. Wilfer was confident that he could produce handmade paper multiples of Close's portraits, if Close could convert his images into a manageable range of colors. Close was somewhat skeptical of the proposition, but he was sufficiently intrigued by Wilfer's ideas to pursue the project.

Close selected Keith as his first subject, and after several months of experimentation, he and Wilfer arrived at a technique of translating the portrait image into a paper multiple. Using the Kodak gray scale as a point of departure, Close selected twenty-two shades of gray, white, and black and assigned one to each square of a gridded image of Keith. Wilfer then manufactured pure rag pulp tinted with pigment to match the twenty-two tones Close had selected.

The actual production of the multiples began with the creation of a "carrier sheet," the background paper on which the image would be built. Then a plastic grid the cubicles of which were numbered to correspond to the twenty-two tones was placed over the carrier sheet and the appropriate color of liquified pulp was squeezed from a plastic bottle into each compartment. Once all the cubicles were filled and the pulp had adhered to the precast ground, the grid was removed and the modular image was left to dry.

Each of the twenty prints and five artist proofs in the edition was created through this same methodical process. Although it sounds relatively easy and straightforward, the process was in fact, Close says, "incredibly tedious and nerve-wracking." Working with the liquified pulp there were countless possibilities for error and uncontrollable accidents. But once exposed to the technology, Close became fascinated by its formal and expressive possibilities. To date, he and Wilfer have translated portraits of the artist, his daughter Georgia, Phil, Robert, and Keith into sixteen handmade paper editions.

Along the way, they have found that there are several alternatives for finishing the images. If left to dry naturally, as was the case with *Phil I*, the surface remained three-dimensional and rather rough. If pressed dry with felt blankets, as in *Keith II*, the surface became relatively smooth. With the use of a fixative sprayed on after the print was completely dry, the colors in *Keith III* became darker and were greater in contrast. And by manipulating the squares of color when they were still wet, as he did in *Keith V*, Close was able to reorient the rigid grid and create a painterly, expressionistic variation of the image. "We discovered that sheerly by chance," Close admits. "We accidentally dropped one of the pieces on the floor before it had dried and began to push it around in an attempt to save it. And as we did that, I thought, 'hmmm, look what's happening, *that's* interesting.' So from the point on, we purposely manipulated some of the images."

A subsequent series of unique paper pieces was likewise born of an accident. In making the multiples, wet paper pulp was inevitably spilled on the floor. As the pools of pulp dried, they congealed into small paper chips. "Initially, I just strung them together, and made color charts out of them," Close says. "But I soon recognized that these dried chunks of pigmented pulp could be used as increments for building images, and we started to manufacture them purposely." The result was a series of paper collages on canvases in which the surfaces take on a new primacy. In an 8 x 6-foot portrait of the artist Jud Nelson, for example, the skin is encrusted with hundreds of circular pieces of paper that project out from the canvas surface like high plateaus on a relief map. In other collages, among them images of the artist's wife, Leslie, and his friend Phyllis, the paper chips are larger and thicker, and the mottled faces have a frozen, masklike quality. These are not especially beautiful or endearing images, but they remain technical marvels that testify to Close's extraordinary dexterity and inventiveness.

Far more successful and engaging are Close's most recent pulp paper pieces. Among these is an 8 x 6-foot image of Close's daughter Georgia. Here, Close began by making a detailed pencil drawing on canvas, rendering the face as a pattern of amoeba-shaped modules. Each of these modules was then numbered to correspond to a

In photo studio with model

range of some twenty hues of gray, white, and black. While it took Close several weeks to make and codify the drawing and "tune" the many tubs of pulp, the actual creation of the collage required only one day. Close explains the process:

The canvas was placed on the floor, and I was lying on my stomach on a rolling scaffolding, a few inches above the canvas—just the opposite of Michelangelo working on the Sistine Ceiling. Joe and four assistants were stationed around the room with numbered buckets full of paper pulp in twenty or so different shades of gray, black, and white. I would yell out the number of the pulp that I needed for a particular area, and someone would reach into the appropriate bucket, strain the pulp, make it into a patty shape and toss it to me. I'd plop it down on the canvas, then they'd roll me to another spot on the canvas and we'd repeat the process with the next color. The consistency of the stuff was like cottage cheese, so I could manipulate it along the way.

The resulting work is an astonishing feat of pictorial invention, in which image and ground, line and color, form and content are neatly conflated within the confines of the canvas rectangle. Although the "pulp by numbers" process by which the image was created was undeniably laborious, the image seems to have been spontaneously generated. And despite the weightiness and density of the collaged surface, there is a sense of liveliness and buoyancy here—both in the animation of the model's face and the spontaneity of the artist's touch.

Close's changing attitudes toward black-and-white compositions are paralleled in his approach to the color images he has produced in the past ten years. Here, too, he has employed a variety of more improvisational methods. For example, he has injected a surprising exuberance into his mechanistic dot technique, producing a series of watercolors that elegantly expose his three-color process. Among these is *Mark Watercolor/Unfinished*, 1978, a gridded image composed of horizontal bands of variegated color. The bottom of the face is a mosaic of reds; across the mouth red and blue combine to form purple hues ranging from pale violets to deep magentas; only the top half of the face received the final yellow overlay to create full color. The luminous image is an unexpected sensuous revelation within Close's seemingly factual and dispassionate art.[16]

In a series of works begun in 1977, Close has broken out of the severe constraints of his three-color system. With an arsenal of pastels in a full spectrum of hues, he has made "pointillist" images on paper tinted with watercolor in delicate peach or green tones. According to Close, "It's the antithesis of using only three colors.

With the pastels, I had unlimited color at my disposal. Instead of spending my time making layers of three colors, the time was spent shuffling through boxes trying to find the right piece of chalk."

This process results in images whose visual and emotional impact is radically different from that of his continuous-tone paintings. A comparison of the acrylic and pastel versions of Mark is instructive. The face in the 9-foot-high painting is a seamless, volumetric form that hovers in space and looms out over the viewer. There is no escaping the subject's mesmerizing gaze, nor the allure of the extraordinarily detailed surface. By comparison, the faces in the Mark pastels sustain more abstract readings, as flat mosaics of shimmering hues. Even viewed from a distance, when the images come into focus, there is little illusion of depth or volume and the chalky visages seem about to atomize into a thousand particles of color.

The pastels mark the beginning of a return to real physicality in Close's art. "In making the airbrush portraits, I never really touched the surface of the canvas while applying the paint. I just waved the gun in front of it, and the image materialized," Close says. "A good deal of the excitement in making the pastels was holding the chalk in my hand, physically manipulating the material, and making real contact with the surface."

Once he had allowed himself that pleasure it was probably inevitable that Close would feel nostalgia for the smell and feel of oil paint. He had abandoned the medium in the 1960s because it had become, as he says, "familiar and habitual, a kind of mindless self-gratification.... And I tended to view my tools as magical. When I got into trouble, I would reach for my lucky brush—the brush I had used to pull off another painting. So to break the habits, to move on, I threw out the brushes, I threw out the palette, I threw out the oils." By 1980, however, "enough water had passed under the bridge so that the medium had become neutral." Nonetheless, he knew that old habits die hard; it would be easy to slip back into "making the old art marks." So when he took up the brush again to paint a portrait of his friend Stanley, he adopted certain limits in his approach. He compares the new technique he developed to, of all things, golf:

Golf is the only sport in which you move from the general to the specific. In the beginning when you take your first shot, you can't even see the pin. And in a matter of three or four strokes, you're supposed to be in the cup, a very small, specific place a very long ways away.

I thought of the gridded canvas as a golf course, and each square

Ray Johnson and **RAY SERIES, 1980**

of the grid as a par-four hole. Then just to complicate things and make the game more interesting, I teed off in the opposite direction of the pin. For example, I knew that the color of the skin was going to be in the orange family, so I started out by putting down a thin wash of blue, green or purple—something very different from what the final color would be. The second color then had to go miles to alter the first one. So for this big correcting stroke, I chose a hue that moved me into the generic color family I should have been aiming for. Now I had moved into orange, but it was too yellow, so in the middle of that stroke, I put down a gob of red to move into a reddish orange. Then I was at the equivalent of being "on the green" and hopefully quite close to the cup. But the color was still much too bright. So the final stroke was a little dot of blue, the complementary color, which optically mixed with the orange and lowered its intensity, dropping it down to an orangish brown. I was in the cup.

By comparison with the rigid and explicit set of self-imposed limitations of his previous methodology, the rules of this painting game were quite flexible. It was possible, as Close points out, continuing the golf analogy, "to have a birdie—to come in a stroke early. It was even possible to have an eagle—to come in two under par. Of course, it was also equally possible to have a bogie or a double bogie, and even to get mired in some aesthetic sandtrap, just making strokes and getting nowhere at all."

Technically and stylistically, the oil paintings are poles apart from Close's earlier canvases. In such airbrushed portraits as *Mark*, 1979, for example, a few tablespoons of paint were sufficient to cover the entire canvas, and the resulting surface has a hard, machined quality. By contrast, the 1981 oil painting, *Stanley*, is a vast field of lush, heavily impastoed color within which the model's features assume new identities as amorphous, multicolored daubs of paint. To be sure, traces of the image's photographic origins still may be detected. But in the separation of the abstract and descriptive aspects of its brushwork, *Stanley* has more in common with the gestural abstractions that Close produced as a student than with his continuous-tone portraits. As the critic Hilton Kramer aptly observed of this canvas, "the marriage of painting and photography that we see in the earlier works...has now been dissolved in an amicable divorce."[17]

Just as Close's painterly impulses have achieved a new independence in recent years, so too have his photographic interests. In 1979 he was invited by Kathy Halbreich, then the director of the Hayden Gallery at MIT in Cambridge, to experiment with the Polaroid Corporation's large-format camera. Constructed of mahog-

any, the camera is essentially an overgrown old-style view camera with a built-in Polaroid back. It operates on the same principle as the familiar Polaroid camera invented by Dr. Edwin Land in 1947, producing 20 x 24-inch instant color prints on Polacolor professional film.[18] Aside from their stupendous size, 20 x 24 prints are distinguished from other color photographs by their vivid hues and high degree of resolution, qualities that were of special interest to Close. The glossy prints, he believed, would make excellent "working drawings" for his paintings, and so he eagerly accepted Halbreich's invitation. A few months later, he flew from New York to Boston, and asked several friends and family members to serve as his models during a week-long photo session at the gallery.

Much to his surprise, Close found his first session with the camera to be an exciting experience, one that had a profound effect on his view of photography and his use of the medium. He was especially intrigued by the camera's instant feedback capability which is analogous to video playback: it allows the artist to immediately see the work he has done. More important, as the photographer JoAnn Verburg has observed, "Feedback makes it possible for an artist to evaluate the consequences of his or her decisions shortly after making them...while the artist's intentions are still fresh in his or her mind....Instant feedback seems in some situations to accelerate the creative process, and in others to actually alter the work. For often, after examining a print, an artist will make changes in subject matter or technique...."[19]

This was precisely the case with Close. As he explains:

Working with traditional cameras I never knew what I had until the film was processed, so I tended to shoot essentially the same photograph over and over again to insure that I would get at least one usable image. But with the Polaroids, I could instantly see my results, and if I got a good shot the first time, there was no sense in making a duplicate. So in subsequent shots, I changed the lighting or the bracketing, or I would tilt the model's head at a different angle, or ask the model to do something different.

As a result, Close found himself creating a series of photographs in which the subjects display a greater range of expressions and emotions than we find in his painted portraits. Some models—the artist Ray Johnson, for example—even smile. But more importantly, in studying the photographs, Close recognized that most of them were not going to be used as working drawings for paintings or drawings. They were not a means to an end, or as he puts it, "merely necessary byproducts of my paintings." They were finished works

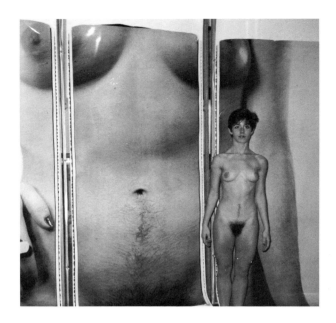

of art in and of themselves. "It was the first time that I considered myself a photographer," Close says. "From that point on, I began to make photographs that deal with the kind of issues I deal with in my paintings." Among these is a group of compelling self-portraits shot with an extreme close-up lens. The most successful and technically refined of them is a composite image in which nine photographs of sections of the artist's face are assembled in a grid composition. Confronting this disconcertingly detailed image is a direct experience. The camera's unrelenting gaze has dispassionately fixed every wrinkle, every pore, every hair follicle in Close's skin. Yet the image exudes a certain poignancy and emotionalism. The artist's expression is vaguely mournful, and his eyes are tightly closed as if he were lost in thought, perhaps even trapped, in some distant reality.

During his stay in Cambridge, Close learned of another, even larger format camera that the Polaroid Corporation had housed in the basement of the Museum of Fine Arts, Boston. This camera produced 80 x 40-inch instant prints, and had been used previously only to photograph works of art. Close convinced Polaroid to allow him to use the camera for his own purposes.

The camera is essentially a room within a room—a light-tight box 12 feet wide, 12 feet high, and 16 feet deep. The subject to be photographed was positioned in the outer chamber in front of the lens and was illuminated with banks of photo lamps. Meanwhile, inside the camera, the artist and two technicians focused the image on a screen against the back wall. Next a huge sheet of standard Polaroid negative stock was lowered in front of the screen. Then Close tripped the shutter, thus setting off the flash lamps and exposing the negative. The negative was then printed by a process similar to that used for small Polaroid photographs. A sheet of printing paper was placed against the negative. The sheet and negative were then passed between a pair of rollers that spread the developing chemicals, and this sandwich was then placed on the floor. Sixty seconds later, the negative was carefully peeled off, revealing the finished photograph.

Close's earliest 80 x 40-inch images included a series of single-panel, head-and-shoulders portraits of friends, as well as a monumental six-panel self-portrait. More recently, he used the camera to return to a subject he had not dealt with since 1967: the nude.

As technical feats alone, the nudes are remarkable. Each model was posed on a platform attached to a forklift truck. A section of the body was photographed, and then the platform was moved to

the left or right, and another section of the figure was shot. The individual 80 x 40-inch panels were then abutted to create figures of titanic proportions. Among these are a pair of five-panel, full-length nudes posed in a manner reminiscent of Close's 1967 painting of the University of Massachusetts secretary, and several diptychs and triptychs of nude torsos.

In selecting models for these pictures, Close refrained from trying to convince his friends to disrobe for the camera, joking, "I figured we'd all probably look like Boteros," referring to the corpulent figures that populate the Colombian painter's works. Instead, he hired a number of dancers whose hard, muscular bodies could better withstand the scrutiny of the room-size camera's merciless gaze. The models are attractive, even beautiful, but they are far from idealized creatures. Through the camera's magnification process, the smallest mole, the tiniest hangnail, which would normally go unnoticed, becomes an inescapable and distractingly large imperfection. Thus, as the photography critic Andy Grundberg has noted, "the subjects seem not so much nudes in the estheticized sense as naked individuals, heroic in size but terribly mortal in their appearance.... Remarkably, they nonetheless seem totally devoid of self-consciousness, naturally relaxed to a degree the viewer is unlikely to share while looking at them."[20] Indeed, confronting these images, the viewer is put in the position of a voyeur and is thus subject to the contradictory feelings of cool objectivity, prurient curiosity, and the embarrassment that such a vantage point inevitably provokes. In 1980 a major retrospective exhibition of Close's art was organized by Walker Art Center in Minneapolis. Touring to three other institutions—The St. Louis Art Museum, Chicago's Museum of Contemporary Art, and the Whitney Museum of American Art in New York—the show generated enthusiastic response from the public and press. Since then, Close has continued to exhibit internationally, and a steady stream of articles, interviews, and catalogues have brought his work to the attention of an even wider audience.

Now forty-six years old, Close is hardly the surly character presented in his 1968 self-portrait. He is an affable, warm-hearted man who, as the critic Thomas Hess observed a few years ago, is "as charming and chatty as his art is tough and mute."[21] He and Leslie and their two daughters—the Closes' second child, Maggie, was born in 1984—live in a rambling apartment on Manhattan's Upper West Side. Five days a week, Close commutes downtown to his SoHo studio, while Leslie, who abandoned the art world several years ago—she obtained a degree in horticulture from Pennsylvania

Opposite page, left:
Installation of *Close Portraits* at The
Whitney Museum of American Art, 1981
Opposite page, right:
Carter with **CARTER/TRIPTYCH, 1984**

GEORGIA/FINGERPAINTING, 1984

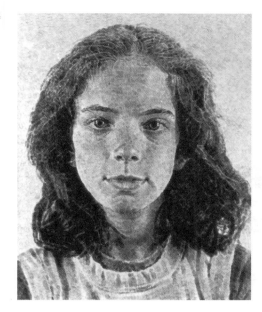

State and a masters in garden history from New York University—drives north along the Hudson to Wave Hill where she is director of American Garden History. Summers are spent at a house in Bridgehampton on Long Island's south shore.

Today Close is more productive than ever. And although he continues to recycle photographs that he made in the late 1960s and early 1970s—Phil and John remain favorite subjects—many new faces, among them Arne, Gwynne, Marta, and Fanny, have been added to his cast of characters. But whether depicting old friends or new, Close's most recent works are imbued with a spirit quite unlike that of his previous creations. If Close's earliest paintings can be described as cool and cerebral, then his latest images are characterized by warmth and passion. To be sure, intimations of these qualities are to be found in his lusciously hued pastels. But in Close's most recent works, we are aware of an increasing urgency to present something more than the surface aspects of reality.

In a recent conversation with his dealer Arnold Glimcher, Close discussed how his attitudes have changed over the years:

Initially I wanted to make big, aggressive, confrontational images. I chose to portray myself as the angry young man, the James Dean period of my life, with the cigarette hanging out of my mouth. I didn't purposely try to make those paintings ugly, but I think there was a certain kind of theatricality there.... I think what's happened is, as I've gotten older and mellowed, I've become more at peace with who I am as a person. I have a greater awareness of and insight as to what makes me tick. I don't feel I need to pose in a certain way as much as I have posed myself and tried to pose other people. I feel much more sentimental about the images.[22]

These new attitudes are clearly reflected in Close's 1986 self-portrait, the first oil painting he produced since completing *Stanley* in 1981. The process he employed to create the image was, he says, "much more capricious and arbitrary" than any he had used previously:

I began by blocking in whole areas of underpainting color in tones that were completely inappropriate.... And in painting the face, rather than arriving at a color in one way, I built the color in several ways. For example, I found that I could arrive at a brown by putting down strokes of orange and blue, or red, green and yellow, or purple and orange. If I could make an analogy for the process, it would be to the way a composer works in writing a symphony. He knows that for the melody line to be carried, certain notes or a chord making one harmonic sound will have to be played. But that chord can be played by any one of a number of instruments. He can build the sound in any one of a number of ways. And the way he chooses to do it will

affect how it sounds and what it feels like. In a similar sort of way, I know what the resultant color has to be, but there is no set way to arrive at it. And it's more fun to arrive at it in a variety of ways and I think it builds a more complex and interesting painting.

The self-portrait is more than "interesting"; it is a sheerly dazzling painting. The artist, clad in a shirt and tie, stares out from behind horn-rimmed glasses. The intensity of his gaze is matched by the intensity of the colors from which the image is built: vivid blues, yellows, purples, oranges, reds, and greens. Prepossessing as the face is as a whole, its parts—dots, near dots, diagonal and commalike strokes of color—are infinitely more inventive—even expressive, a quality that is the opposite of the classic objective Close technique. Weaving across the grid, they fracture the surface of the painting into hundreds of smaller units, each of which functions as a miniature abstract painting, each with its own particular character.

Recently Close has chosen to paint the people to whom he is closest. "The one thing that I realized about this body of work is that almost all of them are women and children. Most of the women are mothers, grandmothers, daughters, with whom I have a personal relationship, rather than art-world friends."[23] Asked if the predominance of female family members in his recent work has anything to do with his mother's recent death, and the fact that he had never painted her portrait, Close replied that "it didn't have so much to do with my mother's death directly, although I suppose I really do feel like an orphan now. I have no one left in my original family. ...There's a sense of being orphaned when your last parent dies, whether you're forty-five years old or five. I lost my father at a young age, and sort of put everything on my mother. She had a major impact on my life, both negative and positive. But if she had an impact on this work, it was that her death forced me finally to figure out who the hell I was."[24]

This soul-searching seems to have had a liberating effect on Close's art. His technical facility has always been impressive; now there is a new sense of ease and a deftness about his touch. Consider, for example, his 1984 portrait of his daughter Georgia, one of a series of paintings in which the image is composed of red, yellow, and blue fingerprints. Because the three hues Close used to create the image overlap, the increments lose their individual identities, and the surface of the face becomes soft and impressionistic, as if viewed through a thin, theatrical scrim.

Then there is *Fanny*, a black-and-white fingerpainting of Leslie's grandmother. "She is the only surviving member of her family," Close explains. "Her nine brothers and sisters, her mother and father, and all her aunts and uncles were killed by Hitler."

As in Close's airbrushed canvases, Fanny is posed frontally against a neutral ground. But all similarity stops there. This is hardly a cold, impersonal mug shot; rather it is a loving and subjective interpretation of the woman's face, whose wizened features convey a life filled with dignity and passion. The painting required nearly four months of labor, yet the image seems to have arrived on the canvas almost effortlessly. And though indelibly stamped on the canvas surface, Fanny's face has the fleeting, vaporous quality of a mirage that threatens to dematerialize at any moment. This is an emotionally sweeping image and arguably one of the best paintings that Close has yet produced.

Although photographs remain the touchstones of his creations, Close has moved well beyond the confines of Photo Realism. From his earliest airbrushed portraits to his recent oil paintings, he has developed a rich, formal, and expressive vocabulary, and his works span a broad stylistic and emotional spectrum. Discussing Close's creations, it may be hard to stray from the issue of technique, because technique is an essential part of his content. But his art involves much more than a display of technical virtuosity. His paintings, drawings, prints, and photographs give evidence of a striking intelligence, a power to dazzle not only the eye but the mind. His relentless curiosity about the structure underlying surface reality and his interest in cool perceptual issues endow each work with special character, and he engages not only the issue of what we see, but of *how* we see. Ultimately, Close's contribution lies in the unique synthesis that his art represents—an elegant fusion of Conceptualism, Minimalism, and Realism. And in this unique synthesis, Close has done more than any painter of his generation to expand the limits of portraiture.

NOTES

1 Unless otherwise indicated, all quotes are taken from the author's tape-recorded conversations with the artist between October 1979 and February 1986.

2 William Dyckes, "The Photo as Subject: The Paintings and Drawings of Chuck Close," *Arts*, February 1974: 31.

3 Thomas B. Hess, "Art: Up Close with Richard, Philip, Nancy and Klaus," *New York Magazine*, 30 May 1977: 95–97.

4 Dyckes: 29.

5 Robert Hughes, "Close, Closer, Closest," *Time*, 27 April 1981: 60.

6 Martin Friedman, "Facing Reality," in Lisa Lyons and Martin Friedman, *Close Portraits* (Minneapolis: Walker Art Center, 1980), p. 13.

7 Leslie Close, in a tape-recorded conversation with the author, May 1980, excerpted in Lyons and Friedman, *Close Portraits*, p. 67.

8 Mark Greenwold, in a tape-recorded conversation with the author, May 1980, excerpted in Lyons and Friedman, *Close Portraits*, p. 69.

9 Kim Levin, "Decoding the Image," *Arts*, June 1978: 147.

10 For a detailed description of the process of creating the mezzotint, see William Dyckes, "A One-Man Print Show by Chuck Close at MoMA," *Arts*, December 1973: 73.

11 Robert Hughes, "Blowing Up the Closeup," *Time*, 23 May 1977: 92.

12 Levin: 147.

13 Ibid.

14 Joan Simon, "Close Encounters," *Art in America*, February 1980: 83.

15 See Philip Rawson, *The Art of Tantra* (New York and Toronto: Oxford University Press, 1978), p. 64, ill. 43.

16 Levin: 147.

17 Hilton Kramer, "Chuck Close's Break with Photography," *The New York Times*, 19 April 1981: 32.

18 For detailed descriptions of the camera's history and technology, see *20 x 24 Polaroid* (Washington, D.C.: National Academy of Sciences, 1982); Susan L. Brown, "Sandi Fellman: Against the Grain," *Camera Arts*, September 1982: 64–79.

19 JoAnn Verburg, "Afterword," in *20 x 24/LIGHT* (New York: Light Gallery, The Philadelphia College of Art and Polaroid Corporation, 1980).

20 Andy Grundberg, "Chuck Close at Pace/MacGill," *Art in America*, May 1985: 175.

21 Hess: 95.

22 "Dialogue: Arnold Glimcher with Chuck Close," *Chuck Close: Recent Work* (New York: Pace Gallery Publications, 1986).

23 Ibid.

24 Ibid.

PAINTINGS AND DRAWINGS

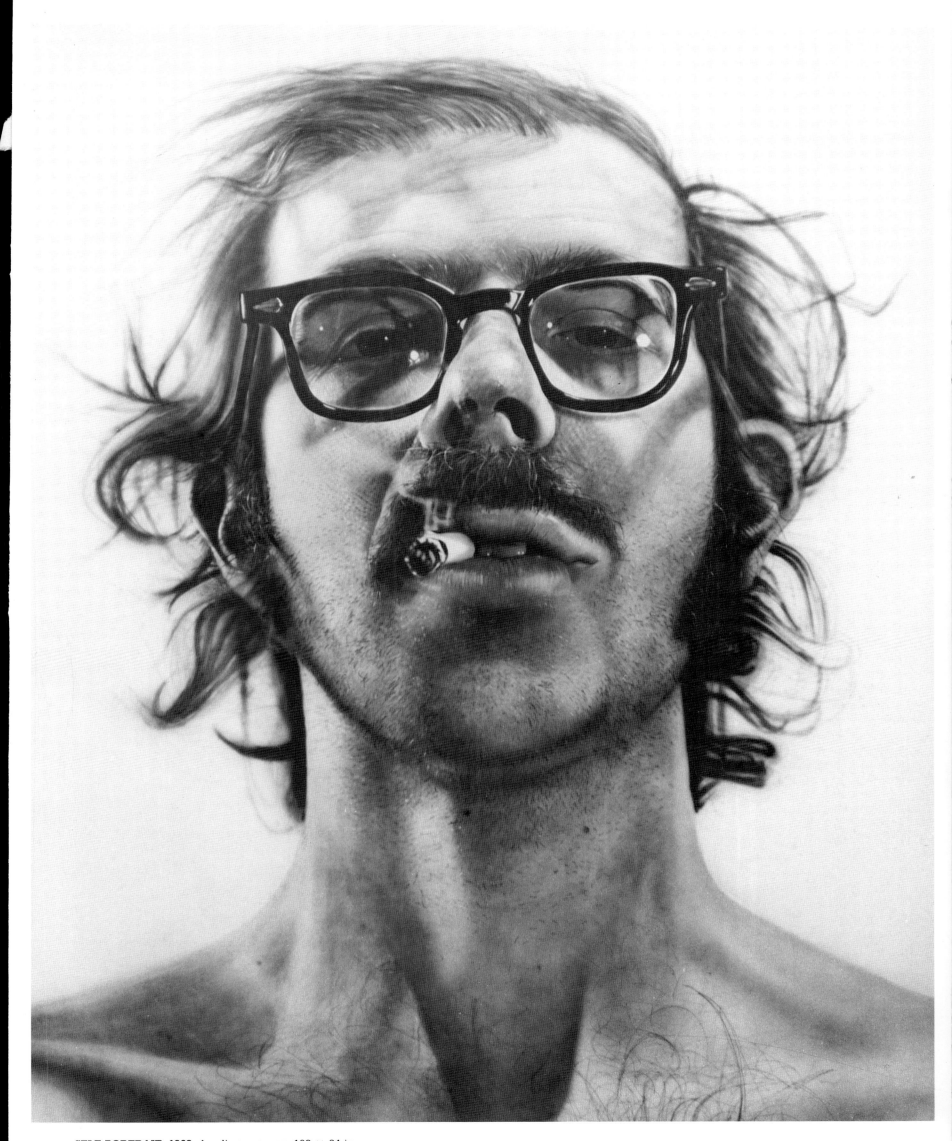

SELF-PORTRAIT, 1968. Acrylic on canvas. 108 × 84 in.
Walker Art Center, Minneapolis

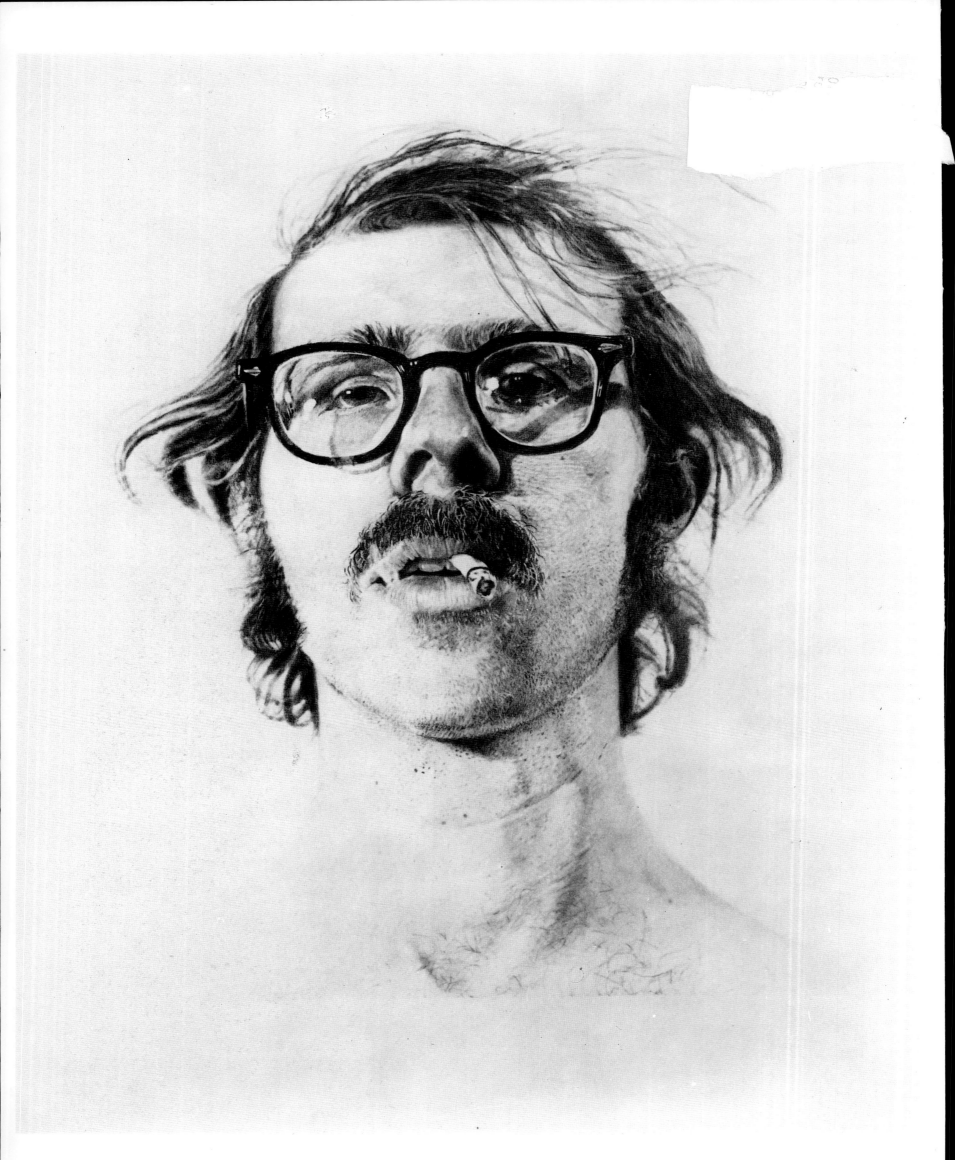

SELF PORTRAIT, 1968
Pencil on paper
Paper size, 29 × 23 in.
Private collection, Boston

Following pages:

In the studio with **NANCY**, **JOE**, and **BOB**

NANCY, 1968
Acrylic on canvas
108 × 84 in.
Gift of Herbert H. Kohl Charities, Inc.,
Milwaukee Art Museum, Milwaukee

FRANK, 1969. Acrylic on canvas. 108 × 84 in.
Minneapolis Institute of Art, Minneapolis

JOE, 1969. Acrylic on canvas. 108 × 84 in.
Doris and Charles Saatchi collection, London

Left and right:
At work on **KEITH, 1970**

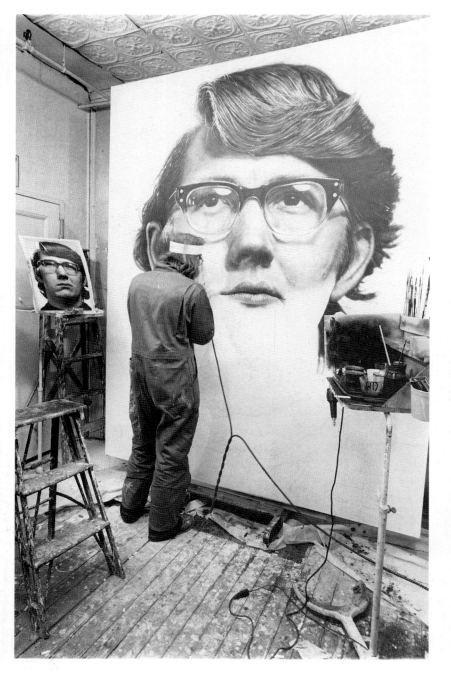 

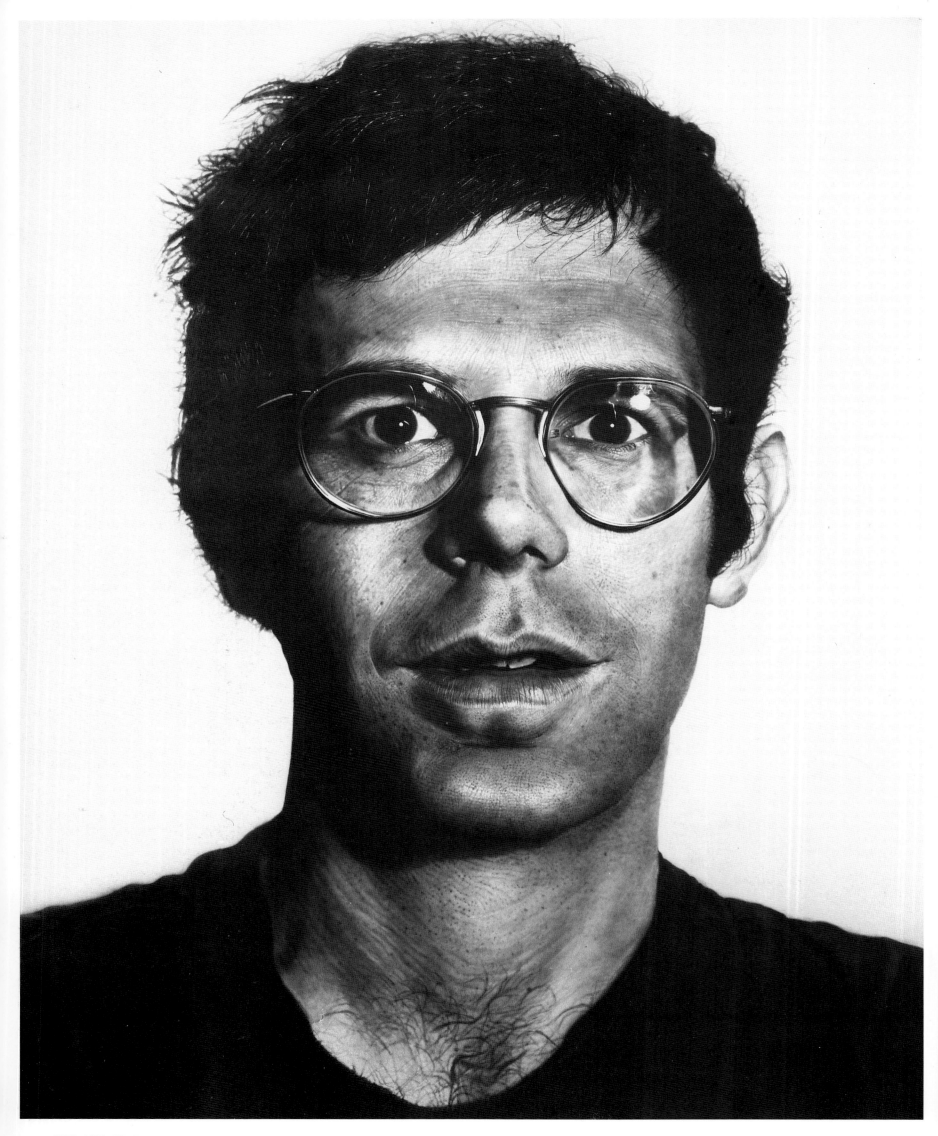

BOB, 1969–70. Acrylic on canvas. 108 × 84 in.
Australian National Gallery, Canberra

RICHARD, 1969. Acrylic on canvas. 108 × 84 in.

Musée National d'Art Moderne, Centre National d'Art et de Culture Georges Pompidou, Paris; Ludwig Collection, Aachen, West Germany

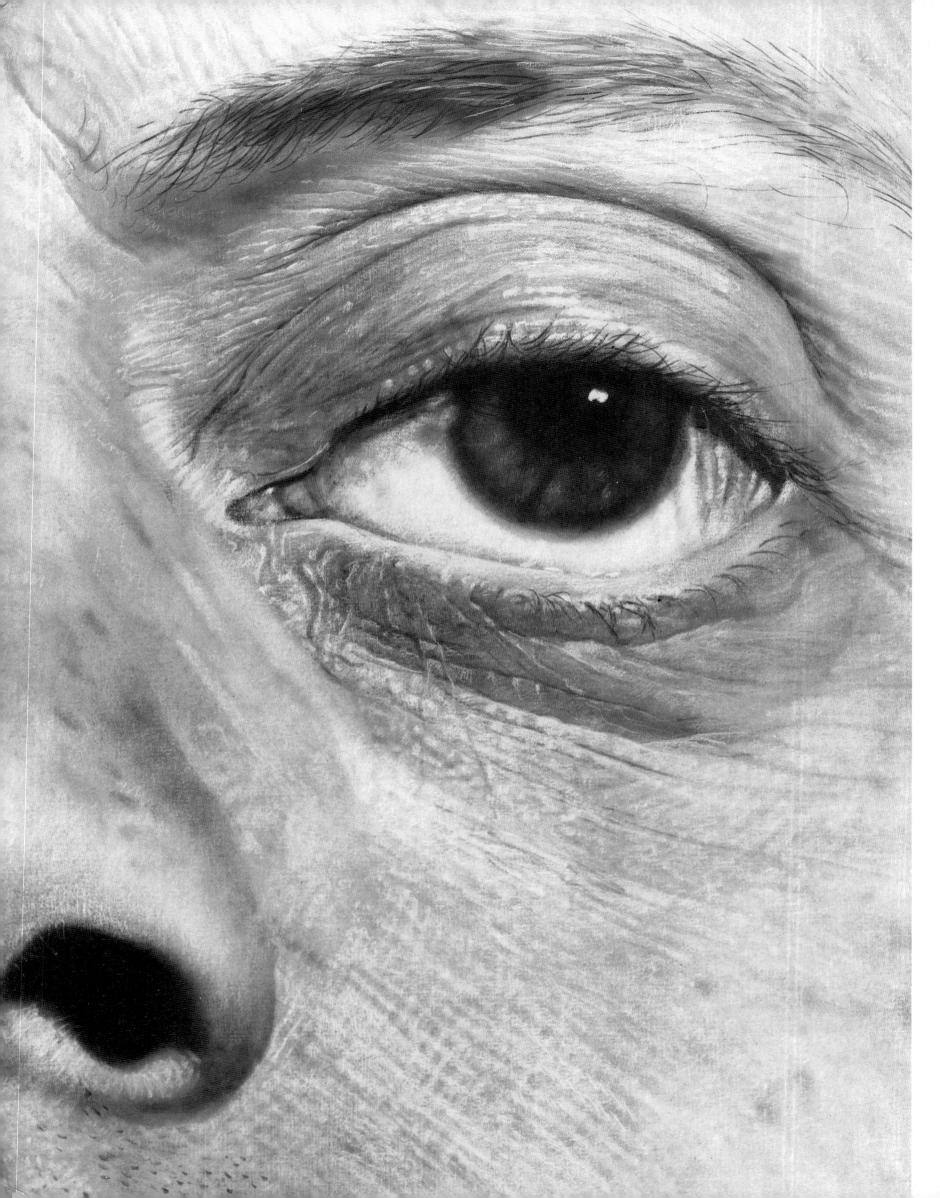

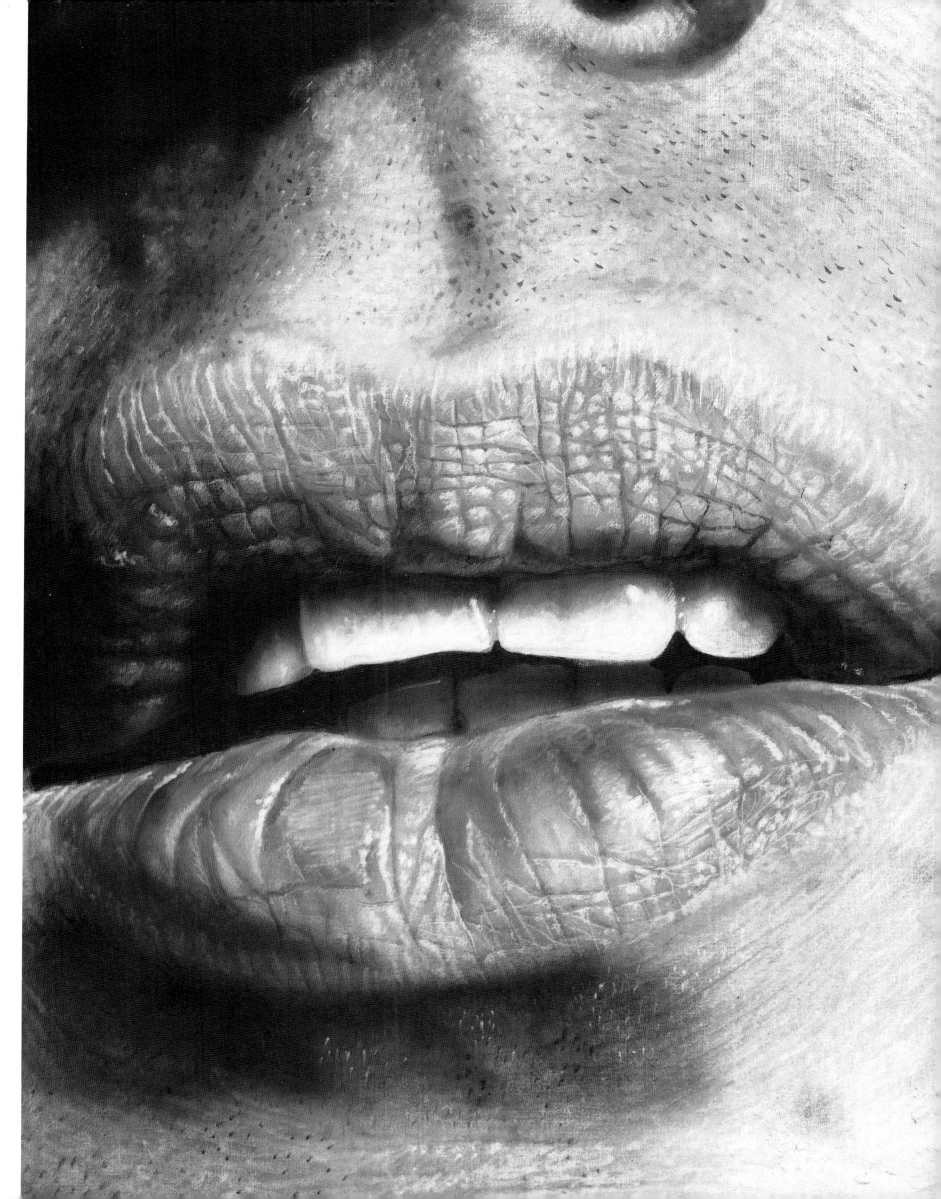

Preceding pages:
Details, **PHIL, 1969**

PHIL, 1969
Acrylic on canvas
108 × 84 in.
Gift of Mrs. Robert M. Benjamin,
The Whitney Museum of American Art, New York

Chuck Close with **PHIL, 1969**

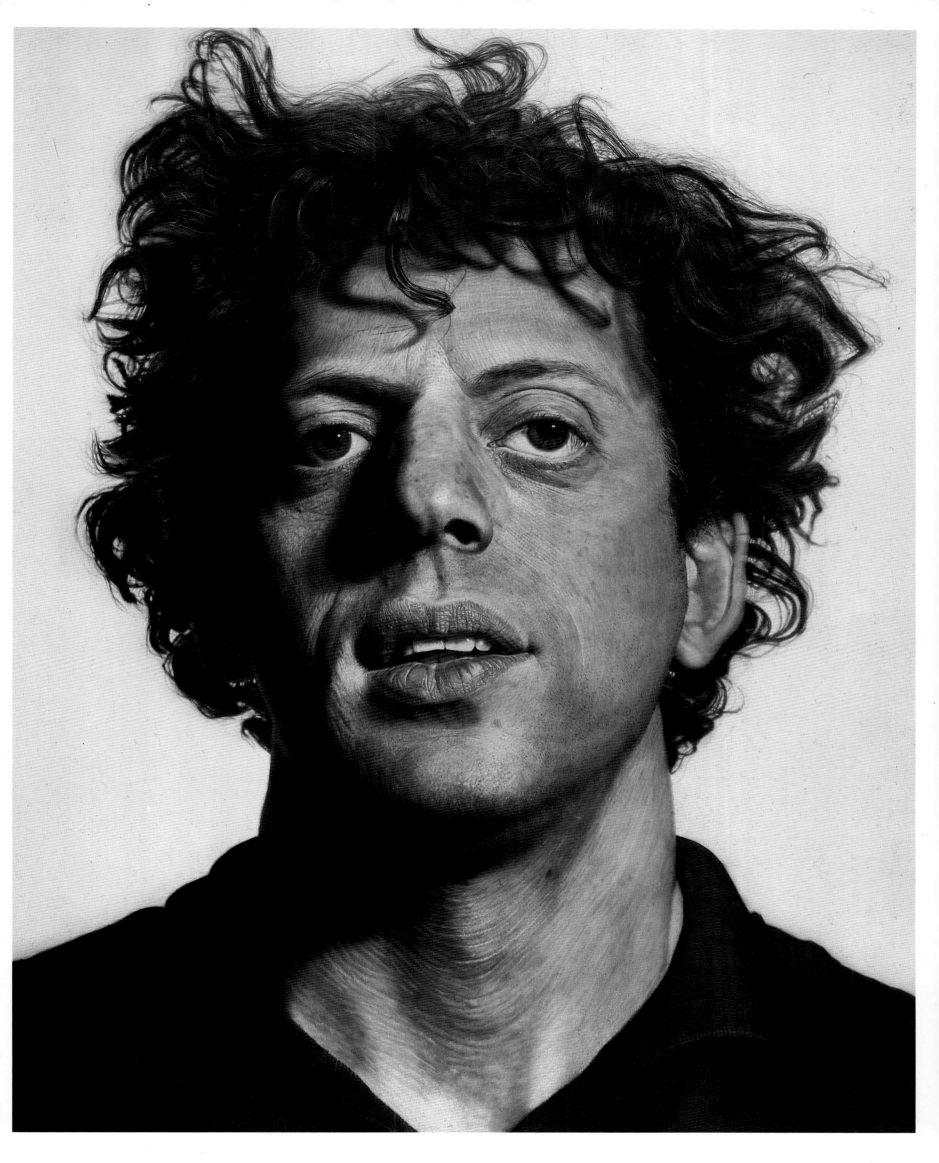

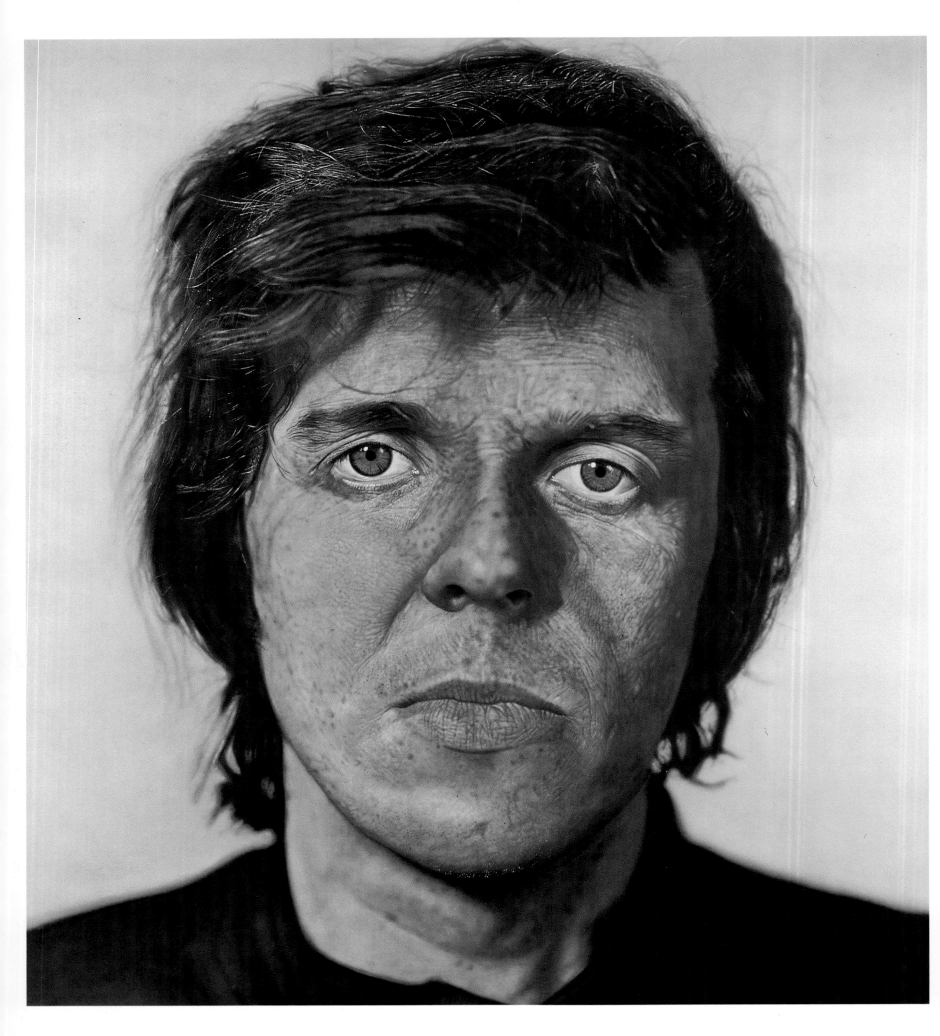

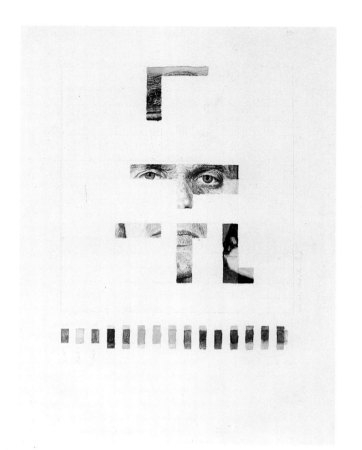

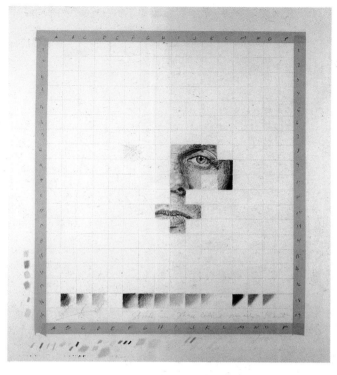

Above left:
STUDY FOR KENT, 1970

Watercolor on paper
Paper size, 30 × 22½ in.
Allen Memorial Art Museum,
Oberlin, Ohio

Above right:
STUDY IN THREE COLORED PENCILS—KENT, 1970

Pencil, colored pencil, and masking tape on paper
Paper size, 24½ × 21½ in.
Louis and Susan Meisel collection, New York

Left:
**STUDY IN THREE COLORED PENCILS—KENT
(Large Kent), 1970**

Pencil, colored pencil, and masking tape on paper
Paper size, 45 × 38½ in.
Private collection, Portland, Oregon

JOHN, 1971–72. Acrylic on canvas. 100 × 90 in.

JOHN, 1971–72. Acrylic on canvas. 100 × 90 in.
Beatrice C. Mayer collection, Chicago

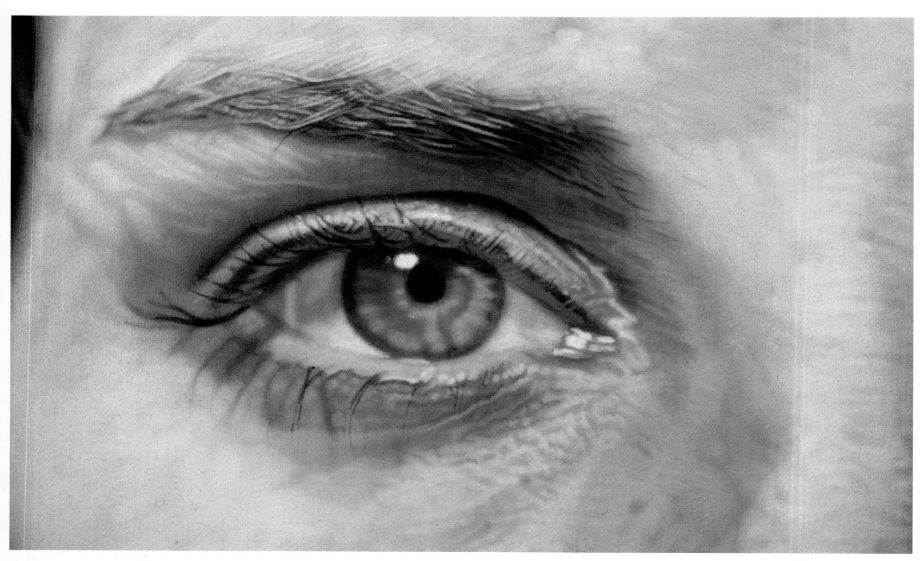

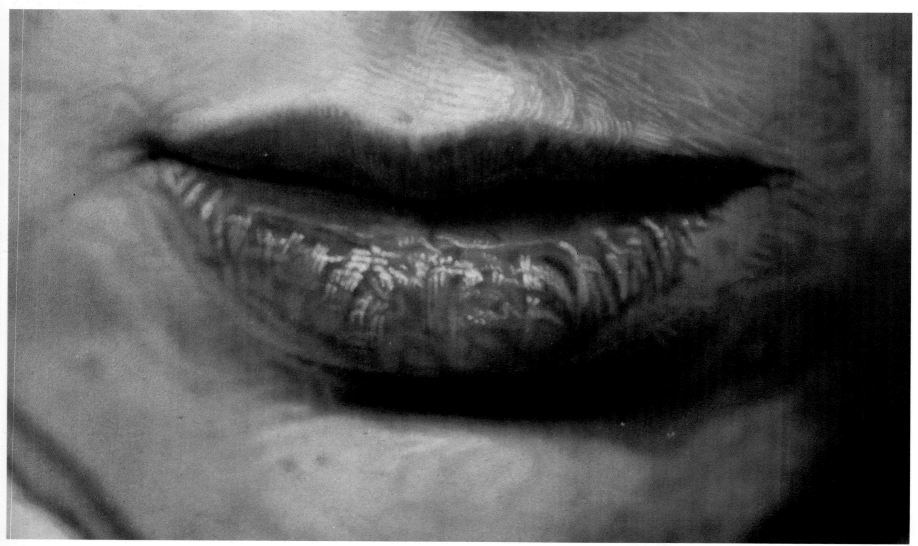

Details, **LESLIE/WATERCOLOR VERSION, 1973**

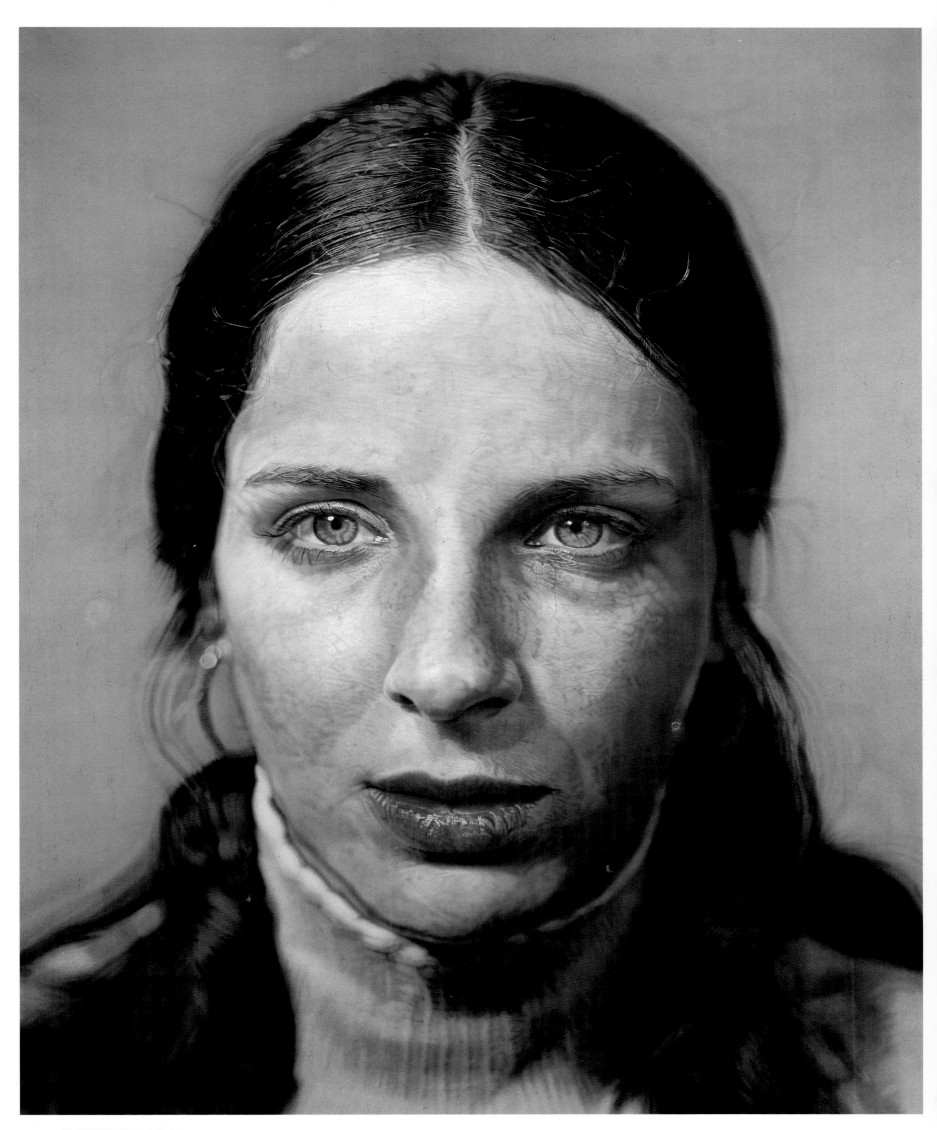

LESLIE/WATERCOLOR VERSION, 1973. Watercolor on paper, mounted on canvas, 72½ × 57 in.
Edmund Pillsbury Family collection, Fort Worth

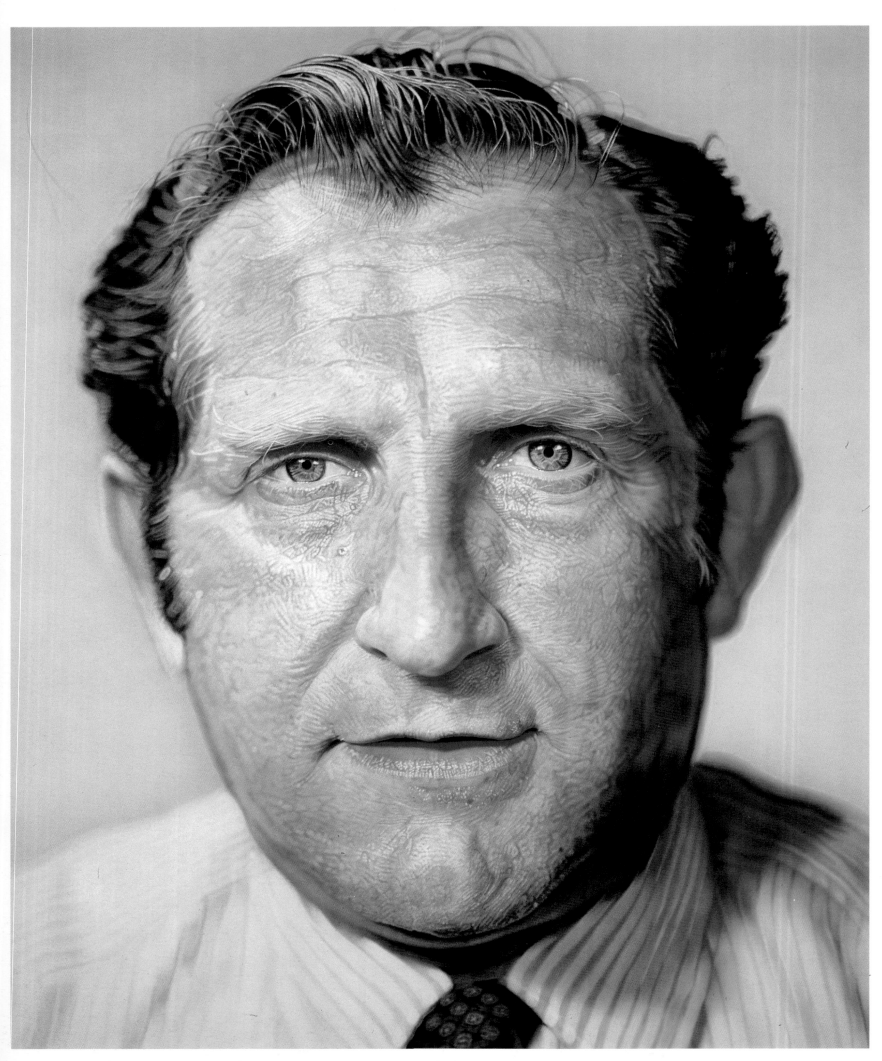

NAT/WATERCOLOR VERSION, 1972. Watercolor on paper, mounted on canvas. 67 × 57 in.
Ludwig collection, Aachen, West Germany

KEITH/1,280, 1973. Ink and pencil on paper. Paper size, 22 × 17 in.
Isy Brachot collection, Paris

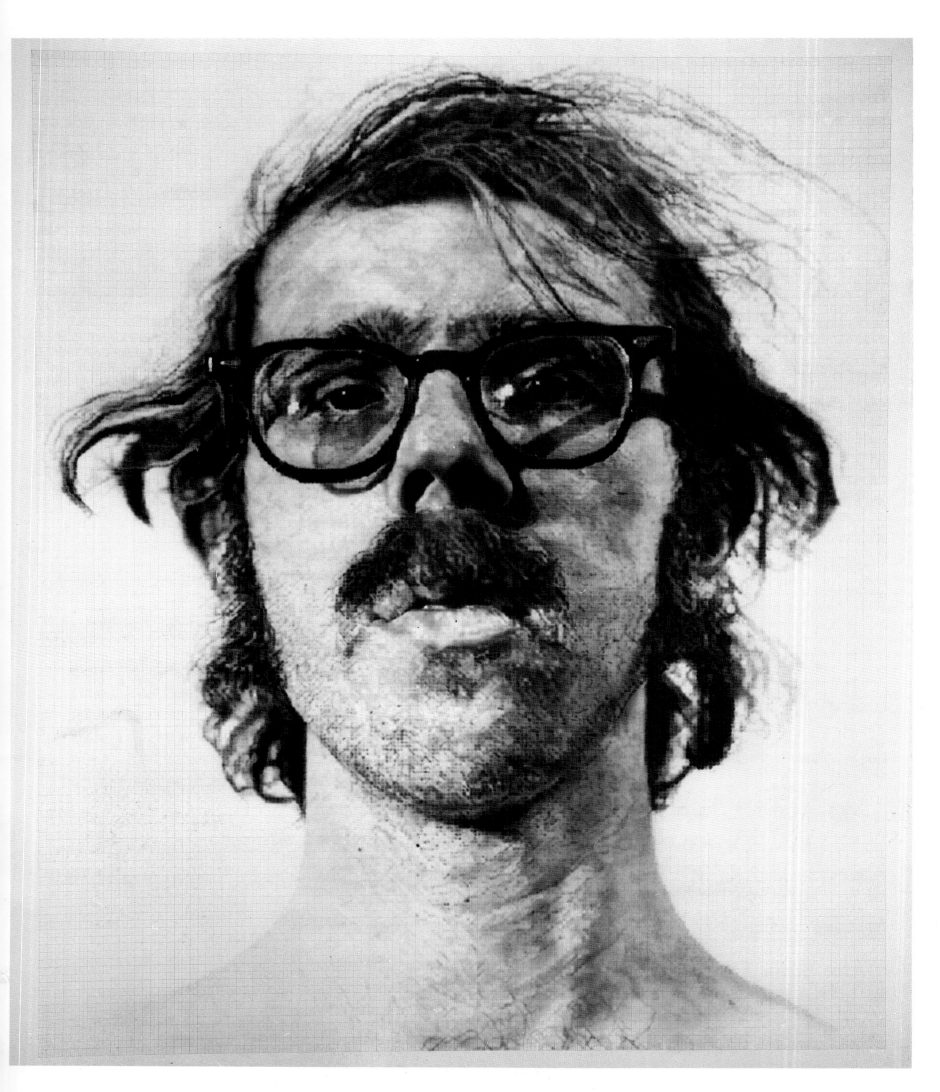

SELF-PORTRAIT/58,424, 1973
Ink and pencil on paper, mounted on canvas
70½ × 58 in.
William Bass collection, Chicago

KEITH/THREE-DRAWING SET, 1973
Each, paper size, 30 × 22½ in.
Private collection

Left:
KEITH, INK ON WHITE PAPER VERSION. Ink and pencil on paper

Center:
KEITH, WHITE INK ON BLACK PAPER VERSION. White ink on black paper

Right:
KEITH, INK ON GRAPHITE VERSION. Ink on graphite ground on paper.

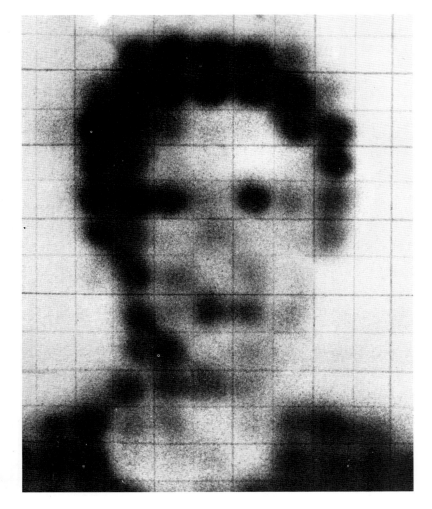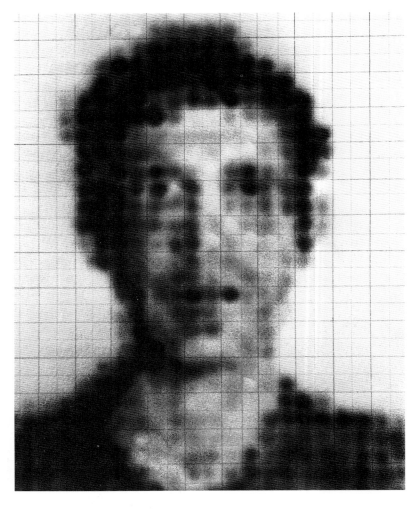

BOB I, II, 1973. Ink and pencil on paper. Each, paper size, 30 × 22½ in. Private collection, Winnetka, Illinois
Above left: **BOB I/154.** Below left: **BOB I/154,** enlarged. Above right: **BOB II/616.** Below right: **BOB II/616,** enlarged

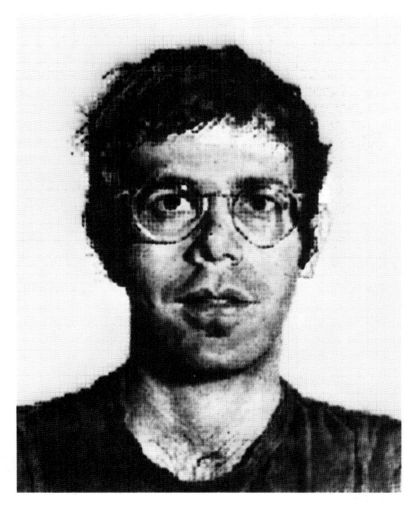

BOB III, IV, 1973. Ink and pencil on paper. Each, paper size, 30 × 22½ in. Private collection, Winnetka, Illinois
Above left: **BOB III/2,464.** Below left: **BOB III/2,464,** enlarged. Above right: **BOB IV/9,856.** Below right: **BOB IV/9,856,** enlarged

SELF-PORTRAIT, enlarged, **1975**

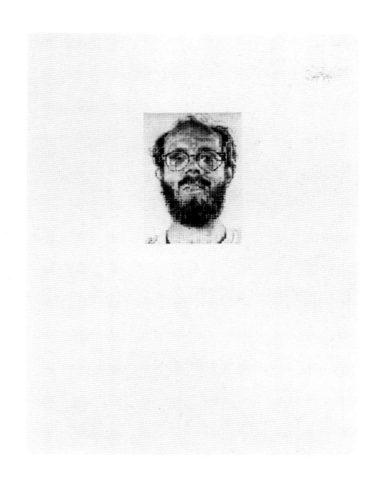

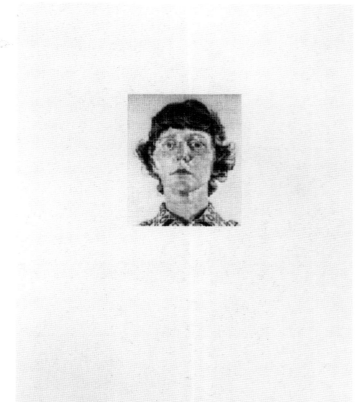

Four drawings. Ink and pencil on paper. Each, paper size, 30 × 22 in.
Above left: **SELF-PORTRAIT, 1975.** Collection of the artist
Above right: **MARGE R., 1974.** Dr. and Mrs. Donald R. Dennis collection
Below left: **JOHN R., 1974.** Mr. Richard Belger collection, Kansas City, Missouri
Below right: **SANDY B., 1974.** Private collection

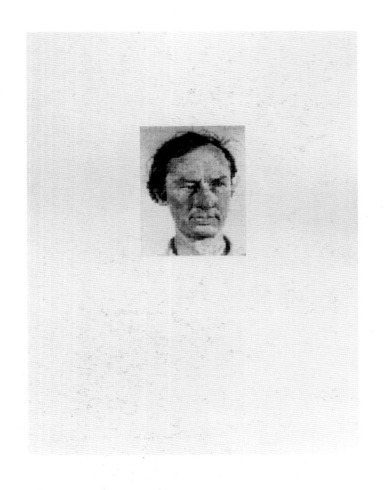

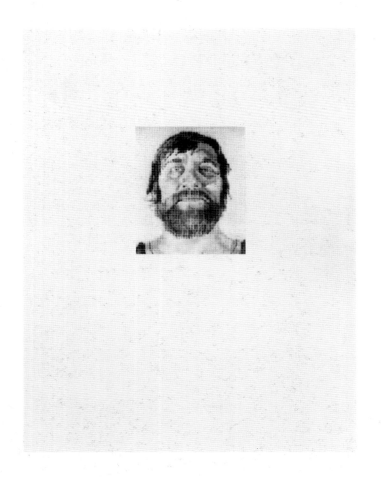

Four drawings. Ink and pencil on paper. Each, paper size, 30 × 22 in.
Above left: **RICHARD A., 1974.** Richard Artschwager collection, New York
Above right: **FANNY, 1974.** Leslie Close collection, New York
Below left: **DAVID P., 1975.** Mr. and Mrs. Harry and Linda Macklowe collection, New York
Below right: **LISA P., 1974.** Edmund Pillsbury Family collection, Fort Worth

FANNY, enlarged, 1974

ROBERT/FOUR-DRAWING SERIES, 1974
Ink and pencil on paper
Each, paper size, 30 × 22½ in.
Tobey Gallery of Fine Art,
Ohio State University, Columbus

ROBERT/104,072, 1973–74
Ink and pencil on gessoed canvas. 108 × 84 in.
Gift of J. Frederic Byers III and the Promised Gift of an Anonymous Donor,
Museum of Modern Art, New York

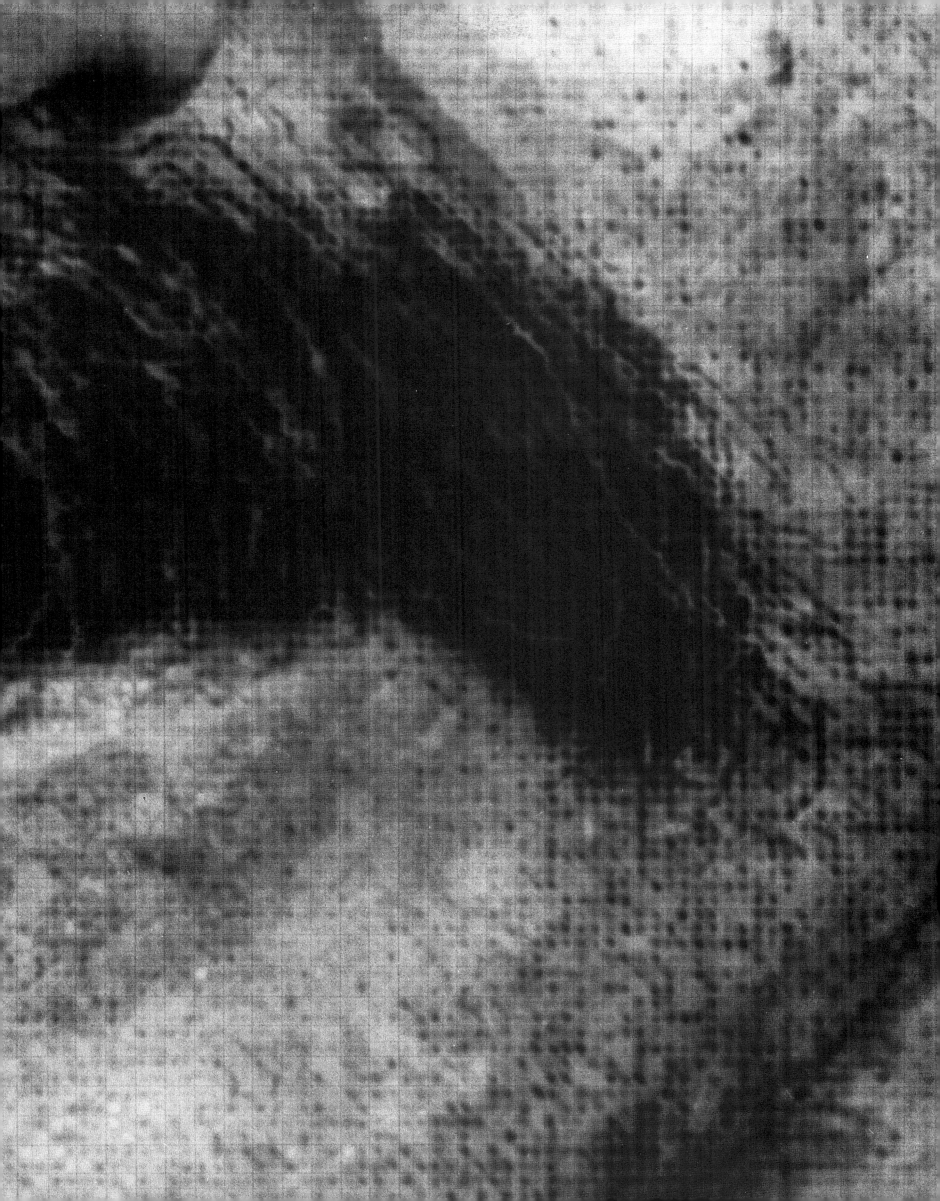

SELF-PORTRAIT/WATERCOLOR VERSION, 1976–77
Watercolor on paper, mounted on canvas
81 × 58¾ in.
Museum Moderner Kunst, Palais Liechtenstein, Vienna;
Ludwig collection, Aachen, West Germany

At work on **SELF-PORTRAIT/WATERCOLOR VERSION,**
1976–77

KLAUS, 1976. Watercolor on paper, mounted on canvas. 80 × 58 in.
Sydney and Frances Lewis collection, Richmond, Virginia

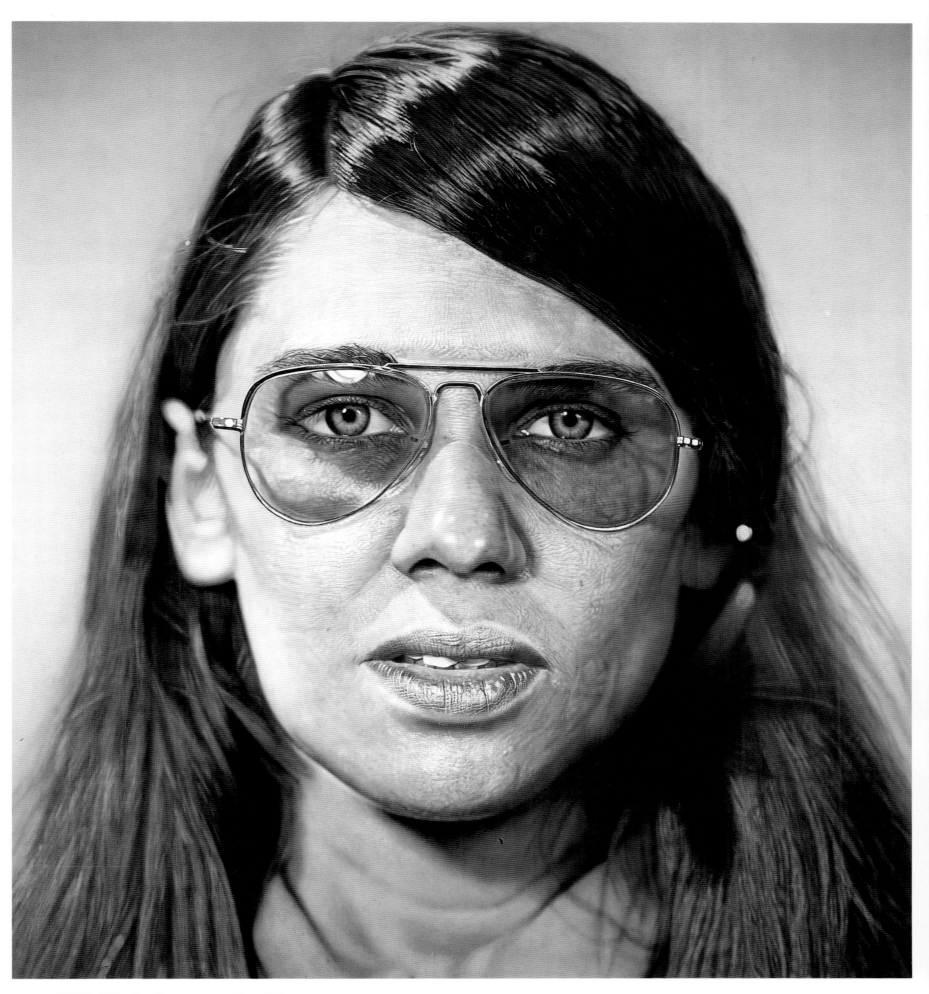

SUSAN, 1971. Acrylic on canvas. 100 × 90 in.
Mrs. Morton Neumann collection, Chicago

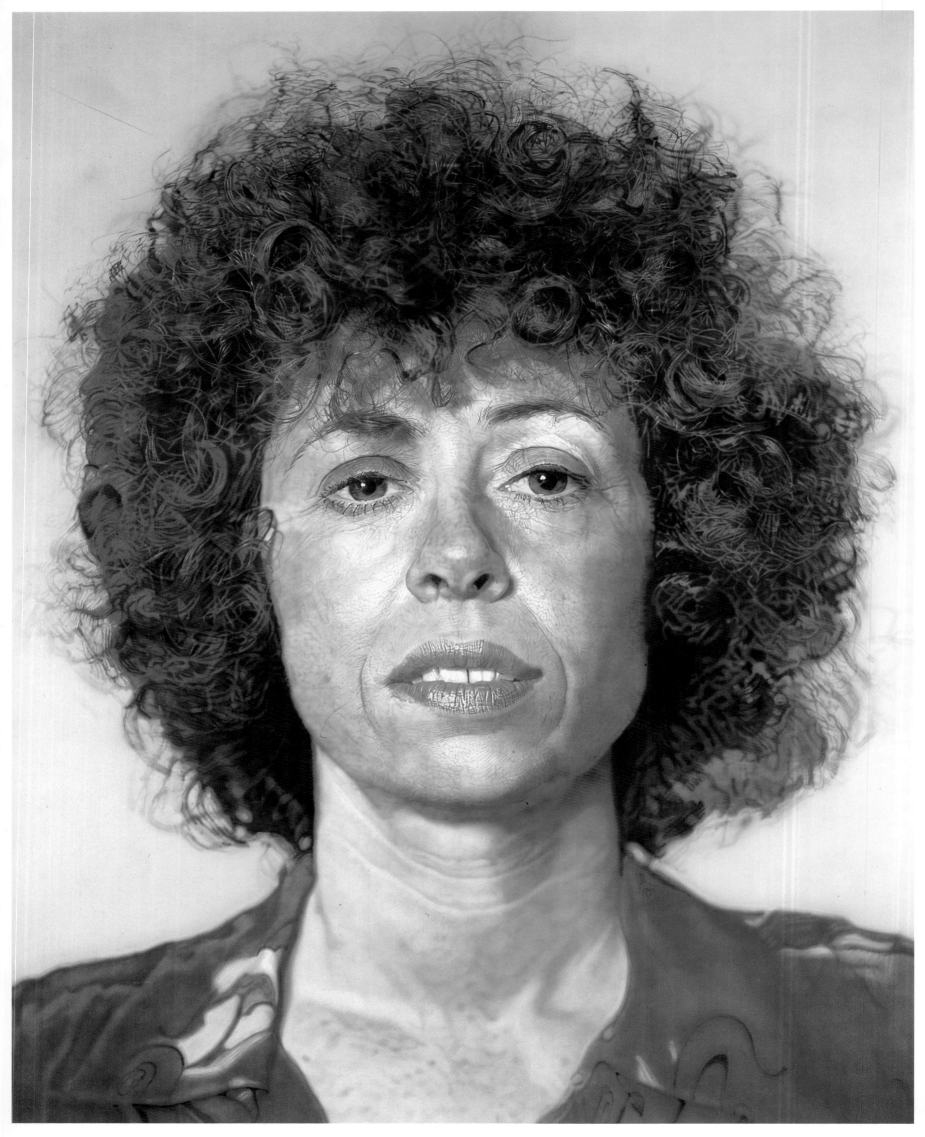

LINDA, 1975–76. Acrylic on canvas. 108 × 84 in.
Akron Art Museum, Akron, Ohio

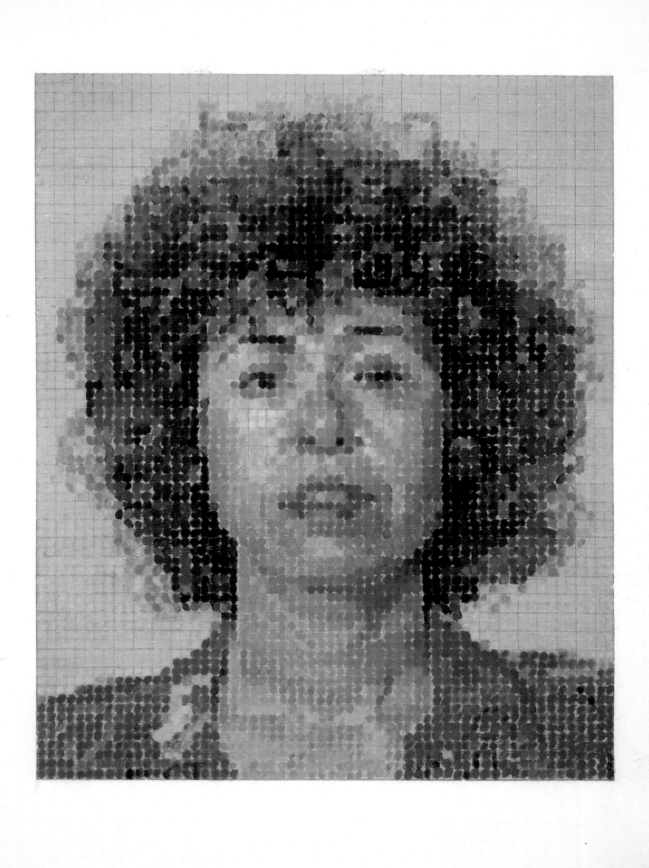

LINDA/PASTEL, 1977. Pastel on paper. Paper size, 29¾ × 22⅛ in.
Private collection, New York

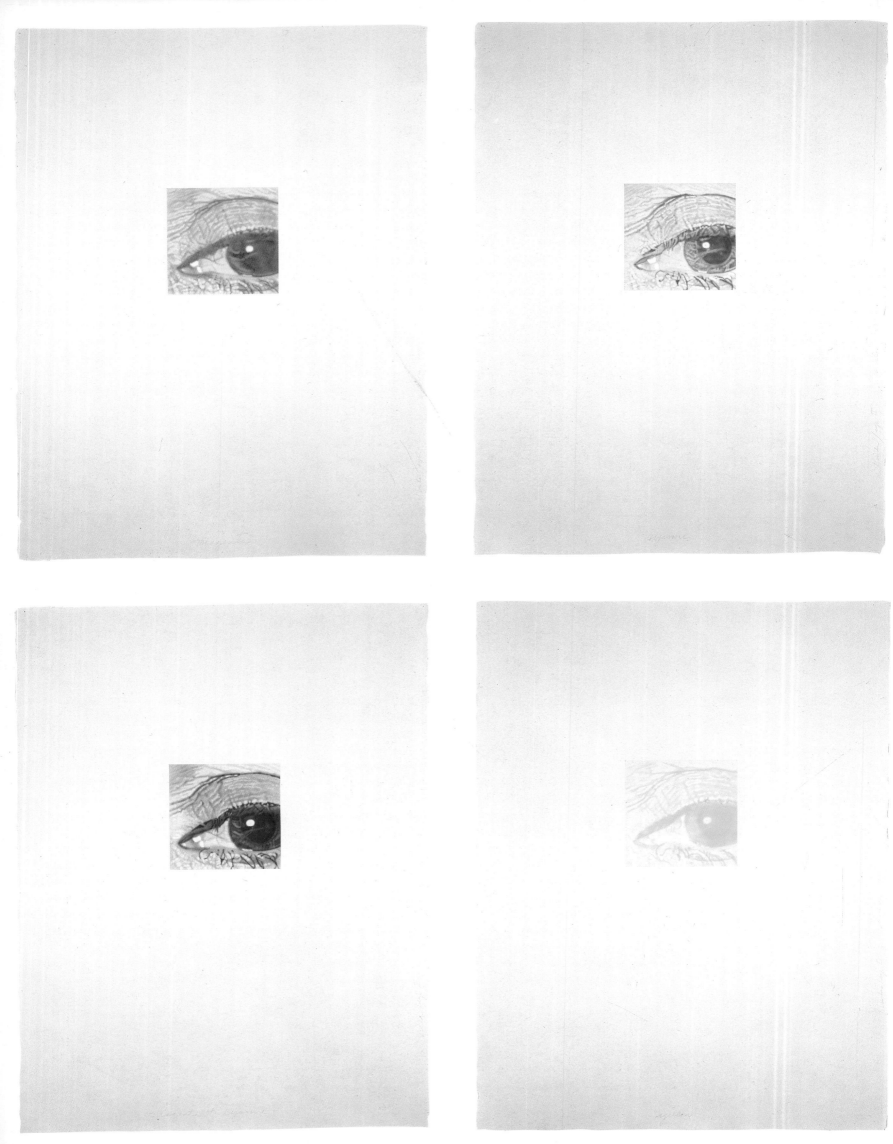

Five drawings from **LINDA/EYE SERIES, 1977.** Watercolor on paper. Each, paper size, 30 × 22½ in. Oliver/Hoffman Family collection, Naperville, Illinois
Top left to right: **LINDA/EYE I—MAGENTA; LINDA/EYE II—CYAN;** Bottom left to right: **LINDA/EYE III—MAGENTA, CYAN; LINDA/EYE IV—YELLOW**

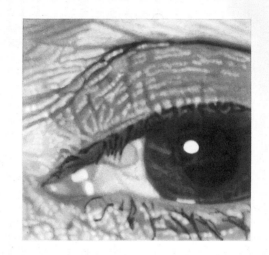

LINDA/EYE V—MAGENTA, CYAN AND YELLOW.

NAT/PASTEL, 1978
Pastel on watercolor-washed paper
Paper size, 29 × 22 in.
Private collection, New York

NAT/COLORED PENCIL VERSION, 1973
Colored pencil on paper
Paper size, 30 × 22½ in.
John Berggruen collection, San Francisco

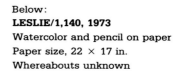

Below:
LESLIE/1,140, 1973
Watercolor and pencil on paper
Paper size, 22 × 17 in.
Whereabouts unknown

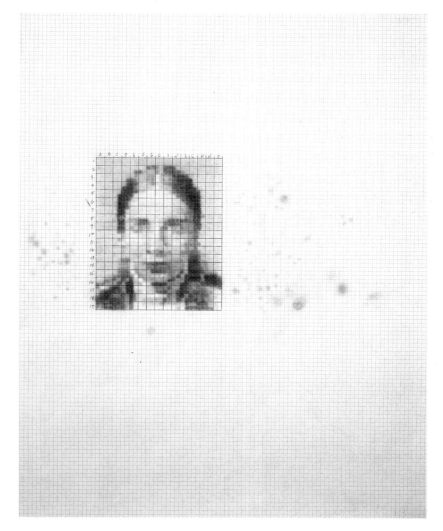

Above left:
LESLIE/PASTEL, 1977
Pastel on watercolor-washed paper.
Paper size, 30 × 22 in.
Mrs. Julius E. Davis collection, Minneapolis

Below left:
LESLIE/4,560, 1973
Watercolor on paper
Paper size, 30 × 22½ in.
Isy Brachot collection, Paris

SELF-PORTRAIT/6 × 1, 1977
Ink and pencil on paper
Paper size, 30 × 22½ in.
Anne and Joel Ehrenkranz collection, New York

SELF-PORTRAIT/PASTEL, 1977
Pastel on ink-washed paper
Paper size, 30 × 22 in.
Sydney and Frances Lewis Foundation, Washington, D.C.

Three **ROBERT/FINGERPRINT** drawings, **1978**
Stamp-pad ink and pencil on paper
Each, paper size, 30 × 22½ in.

Above:
ROBERT/FINGERPRINT
Ackland Art Museum, University of North Carolina, Chapel Hill

Above right:
ROBERT/SQUARE FINGERPRINT I
Julie Auger collection, Aspen, Colorado

Below right:
ROBERT/SQUARE FINGERPRINT II
Mrs. Julius E. Davis collection, Minneapolis

SELF-PORTRAIT/CONTÉ CRAYON, 1979. Conté crayon on paper. Paper size, 29½ × 22 in.
Private collection, New York

Installation of **PHIL** series at the Walker Art Center,
Minneapolis, for the exhibition *Close Portraits*, 1980

PHIL

Among Close's favorite subjects is the composer Philip Glass,
whose portrait he first painted in 1969. Since then he has recycled
the image of Phil more than twenty times, finding that its
complex array of shadows, highlights, eccentric shapes, and
edges, allows for extensive formal invention in a wide range of
media. The resulting works, a selection of which is reproduced on
the following pages, form a virtual lexicon of his styles and
techniques.

Close's fascination with this single image extends far beyond his
ability to "figure out just how many ways there are to skin a cat."
What does interest him is "plugging the same image through a
variety of systems and seeing how it affects its looks . . . seeing
how subtle shifts in materials, devices, and attitudes can make
drastic differences in how the image is perceived." Thus, over the
years, Phil's face has been dissolved and reconstituted as
matrices of airbrushed dots, Rorschach-like inkblots, febrile
diagonal hatchings, crusty clumps of pigmented pulp, and
stamped impressions of Close's fingerprints.

The artist's absorption with the composer's image seems
thoroughly appropriate not only because Close admires Glass's
music, but also because an analogy may be drawn between their
work. As the art historian Robert Rosenblum has noted, Glass's
music is composed of what initially may seem monotonous,
repetitive tones, electronically amplified in a way that nearly
conceals personal style. Yet the experience of listening becomes
a kind of slow immersion in a sonic sea where the structural
anchors of the score tend to be washed away by the mounting
sensuous force of the cumulative sound.* Similarly, by means of
almost mechanical repetition of simple, predetermined forms,
Close creates works of mind-bending intricacy, which, for all
their cool rationality and precision, are loaded with expressive
force.

L.L.

*Robert Rosenblum, ''Notes on Sol LeWitt,'' in Alicia Legg, ed., Sol LeWitt
(New York: The Museum of Modern Art, 1978), p. 20.

PHIL III, 1982. Handmade pulp paper edition (on black paper). Paper size, 69 × 53½ in. Edition: 15

Drawing for **PHIL/RUBBERSTAMP, 1976.** Ink on paper. Paper size, 7⅝ × 6½ in.
Richard and Peggy Danziger collection, New York

Below:
PHIL/WATERCOLOR, 1977
Watercolor on paper
Paper size, 58 × 40 in.
Mrs. Julius E. Davis collection, Minneapolis

Above right:
PHIL/FINGERPRINT, 1978
Stamp-pad ink and pencil on paper
Paper size, 30 × 22¼ in.
Mr. and Mrs. Roger Felderbaum collection, New York

Below right:
PHIL/FINGERPRINT II, 1978
Stamp-pad ink and pencil on paper
Paper size, 30 × 22¼
The Whitney Museum of American Art, New York

PHIL, 1980. Ink and pencil on paper. Paper size, 29½ × 22¼ in.
Private collection, Troy, Michigan

PHIL/2,464, 1973
Ink and pencil on paper
Paper size, 22 × 17 in.
Gift of Lily Auchincloss in honor of John I. H. Baur,
The Whitney Museum of American Art, New York

PHIL, 1980
Stamp-pad ink on gray paper
Paper size, 15¾ × 11½ in.
Jeffrey Hoffeld collection, New York

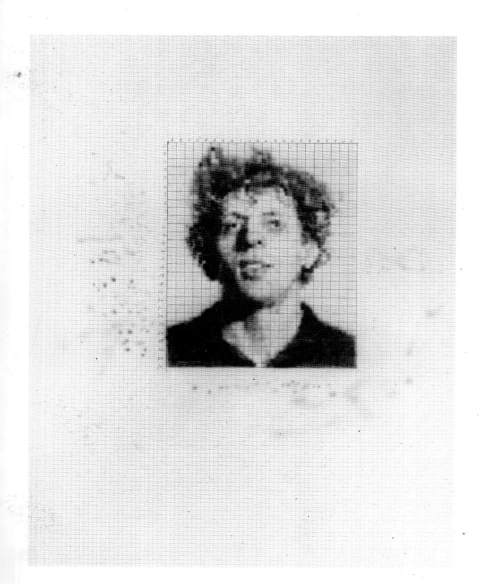

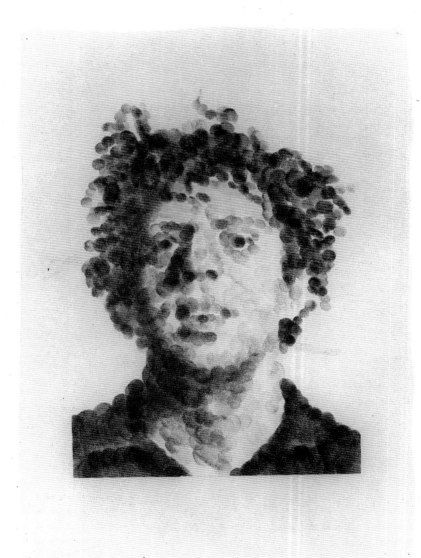

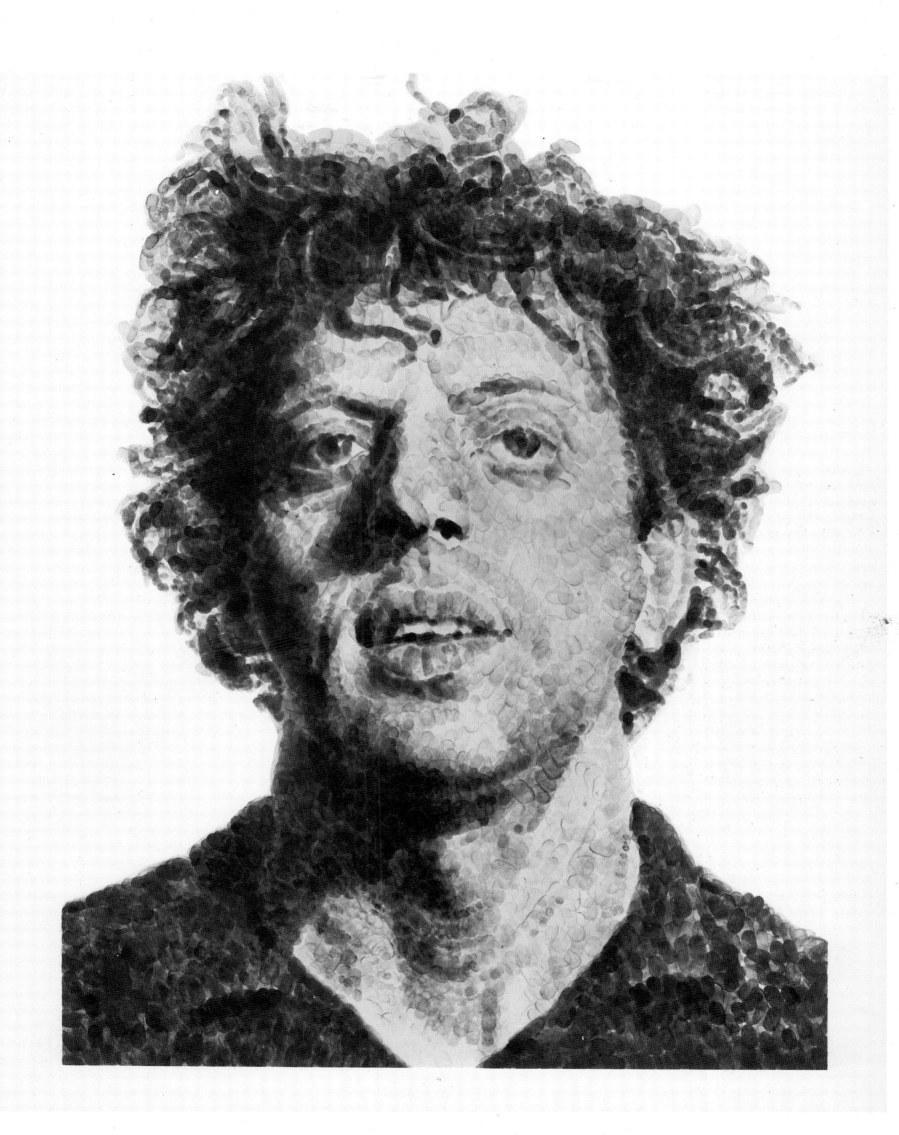

PHIL, 1983
Pulp paper on canvas
92⅛ × 72⅛ in.
Museum of Art, Fort Lauderdale

PHIL FINGERPRINT/RANDOM, 1979
Stamp-pad ink on paper
Paper size, 40 × 26 in.
Seattle Art Museum, Seattle,
Gift of the American Art Foundation

PHIL/FINGERPRINT, 1980
Stamp-pad ink on paper
Paper size, 93 × 69 in.
The Chase Manhattan Bank collection, New York

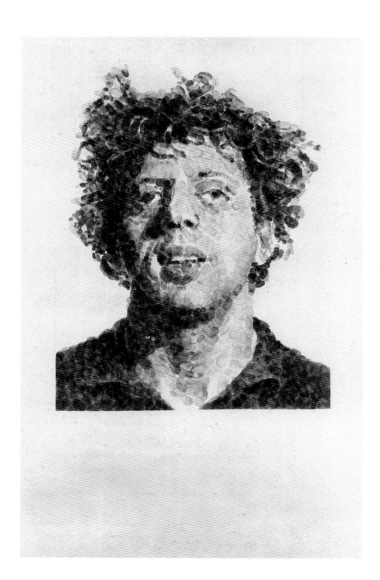

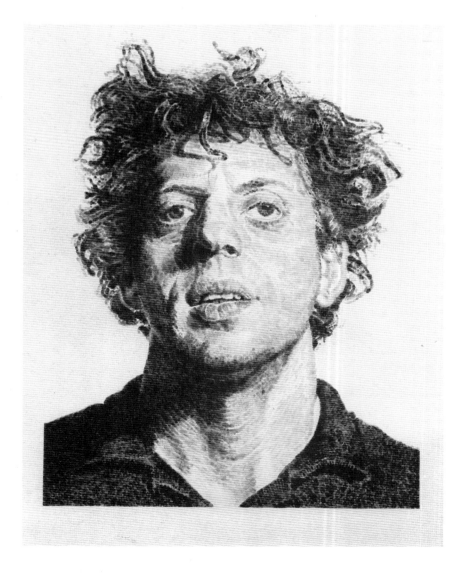

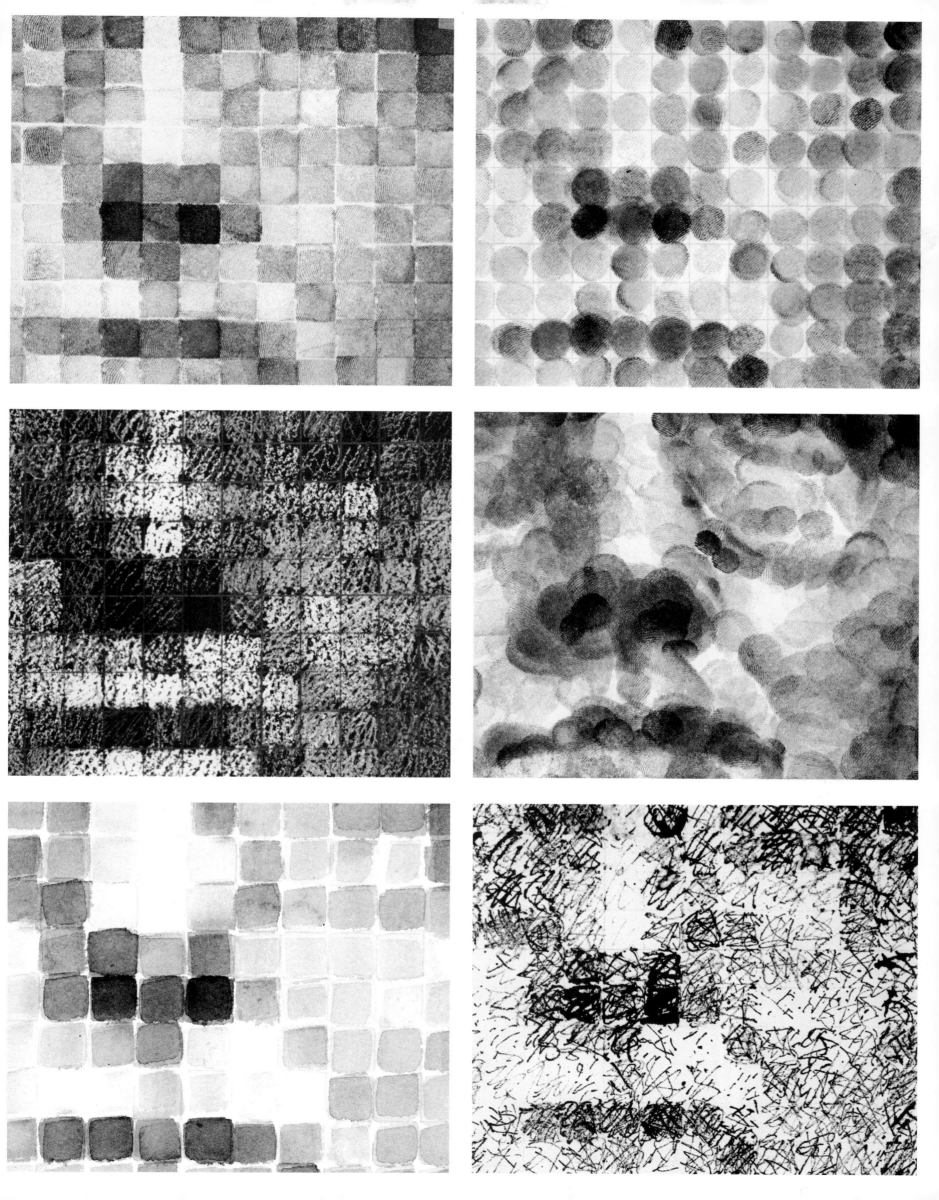

Page 102:
KEITH/SIX-DRAWING SERIES, 1979
Each, paper size, 29½ × 22 in.
Renalda House collection, Winston Salem
Above left: **KEITH/SQUARE FINGERPRINT VERSION**
Stamp-pad ink on paper
Above right: **KEITH/ROUND FINGERPRINT VERSION**
Stamp-pad ink on paper
Center left: **KEITH/WHITE CONTÉ VERSION**
White conté crayon on paper with black watercolor wash
Center right: **KEITH/RANDOM FINGERPRINT VERSION**
Stamp-pad ink on paper
Below left: **KEITH/WATERCOLOR VERSION**
Watercolor and pencil on paper
Below right: **KEITH/INK STICK VERSION**
Ink on paper

Page 103:
Detail of each drawing,
KEITH/SIX-DRAWING SERIES, 1979

MARK WATERCOLOR/UNFINISHED, 1978
Watercolor on paper.
Paper size, 53½ × 40½ in.
Sydney and Frances Lewis collection, Richmond, Virginia

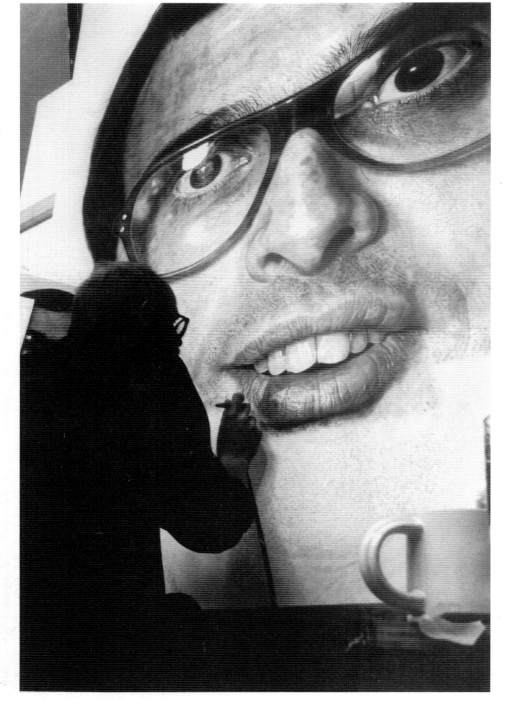

At work on **MARK**, 1978–79

MARK, 1978–79. Acrylic on canvas. 108 × 84 in.
Collection of the artist

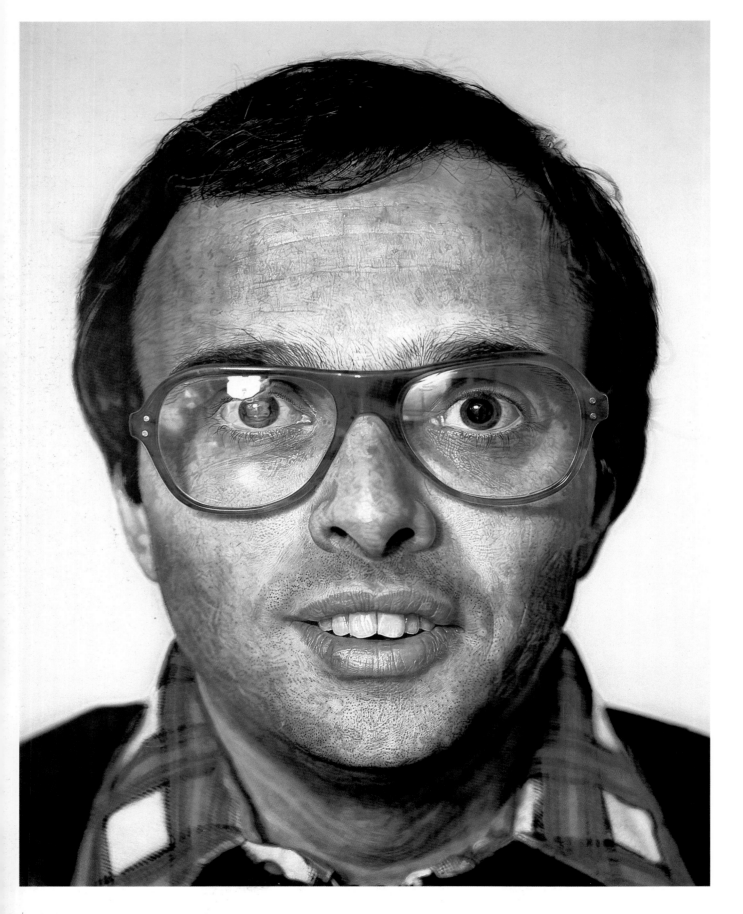

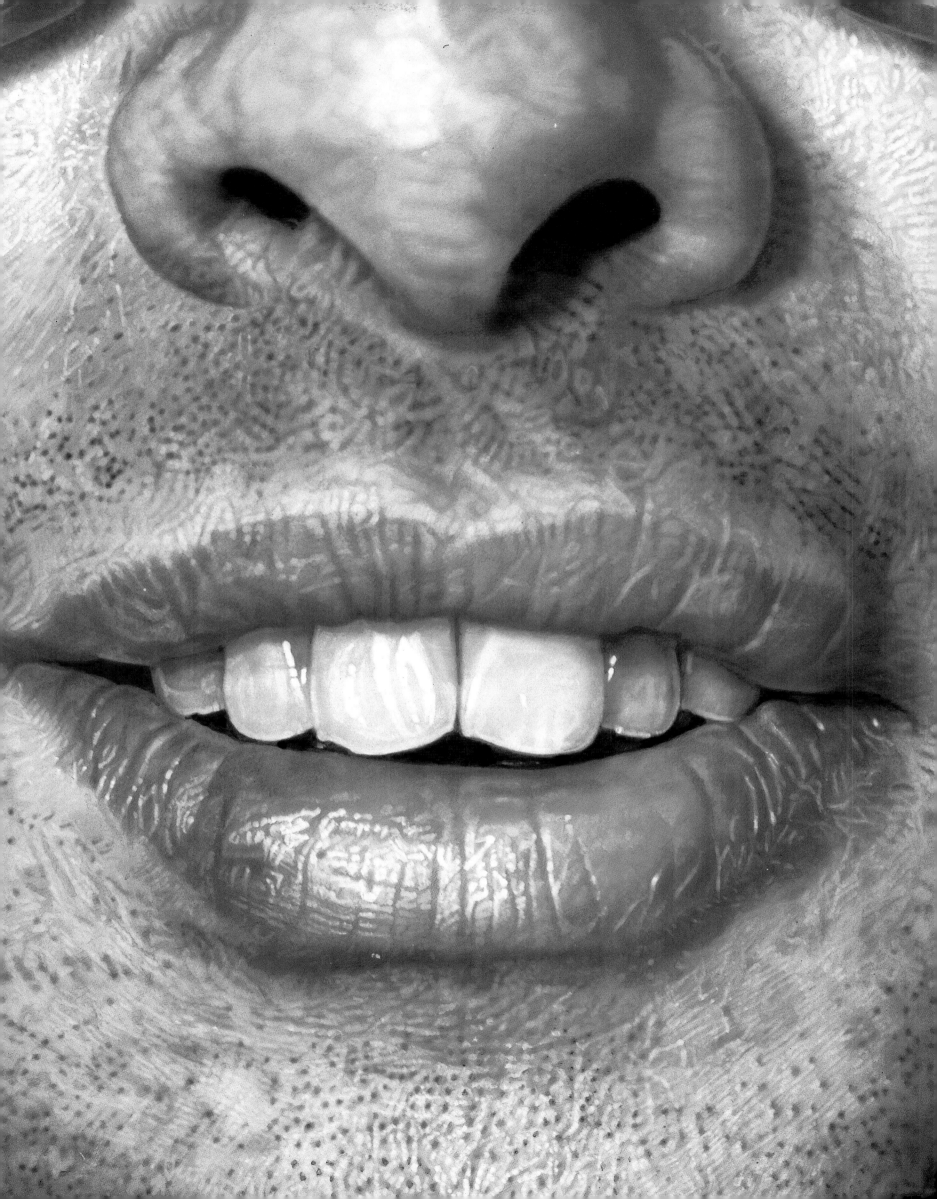

At work on **LARGE MARK/PASTEL, 1978–79**

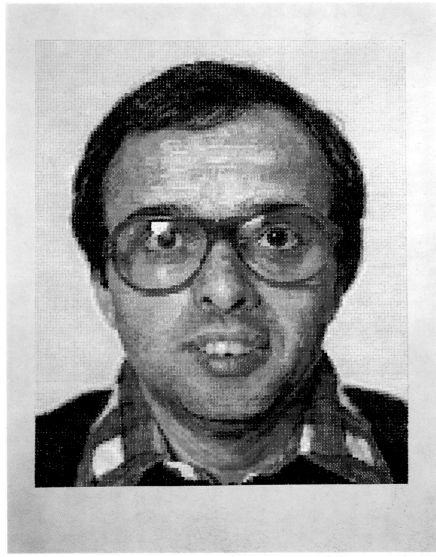

MARK/PASTEL (small version), 1977
Pastel on watercolor-washed paper
Paper size, 30½ × 22 in.
Mrs. E.A. Bergman collection, Chicago

LARGE MARK/PASTEL, 1978–79
Pastel on watercolor on paper
Paper size, 56 × 44 in.
Arnold and Millie Glimcher collection, New York

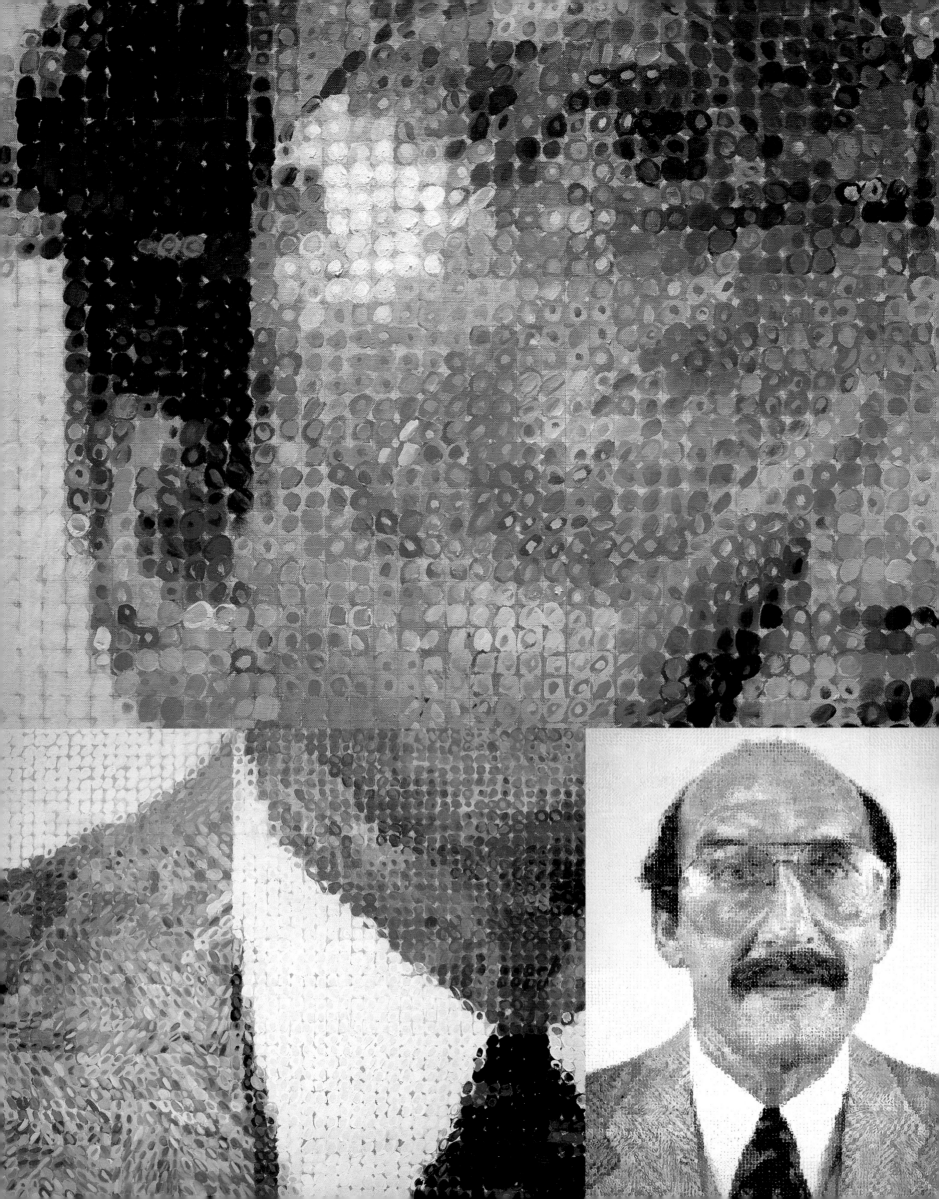

Pages 110-111:
STANLEY (large version), 1980–81, and details
Oil on canvas
101 × 84 in.
The Solomon R. Guggenheim Museum, New York

STANLEY (small version), 1980
Oil on canvas
55 × 42 in.
Mr. and Mrs. Charles M. Diker collection, New York

ARNE, 1980
Stamp-pad ink on gray paper
Paper size, 42 × 30½ in.
The Pace Gallery, New York

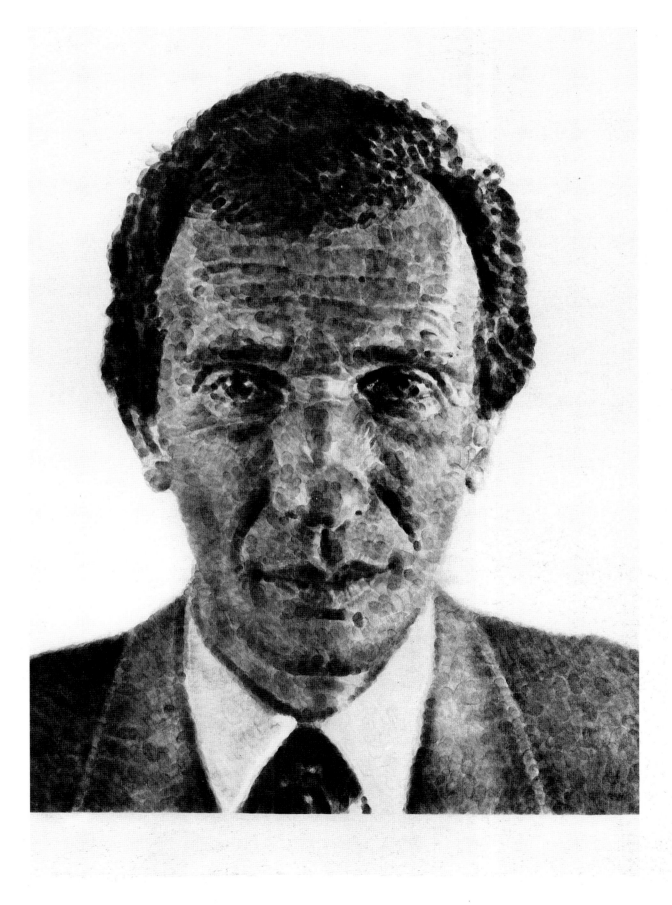

SELF-PORTRAIT, 1980. Stamp-pad ink on gray paper. Paper size, 15¾ × 11½ in. Lisa Lyons collection, Minneapolis

FRANK, 1980. Stamp-pad ink on gray paper. Paper size, 15¾ × 11½ in. Barbaralee Diamonstein/Spielvogel collection, New York

ROBERT, 1980. Stamp-pad ink on gray paper. Paper size, 15¾ × 11½ in.
Arnold and Millie Glimcher collection, New York

GWYNNE, 1981
Stamp-pad ink on paper
Paper size, 43¼ × 30¼ in.
Mrs. Glen C. Janss, Sun Valley, Idaho

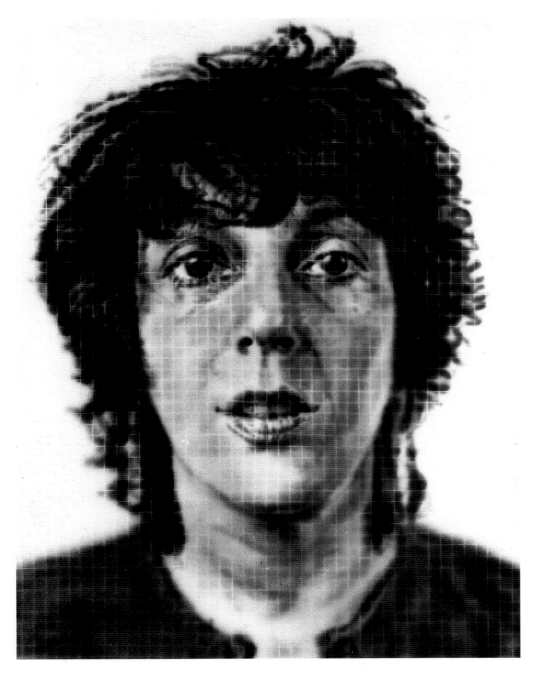

GWYNNE, 1981
Watercolor on paper
Paper size, 29¾ × 22½ in.
PieperPower Companies, Inc., Milwaukee

GWYNNE, 1982
Watercolor on paper
Paper size, 74¼ × 58¼ in.
Mr. and Mrs. David Pincus collection, Philadelphia

At work on **GWYNNE, 1982**

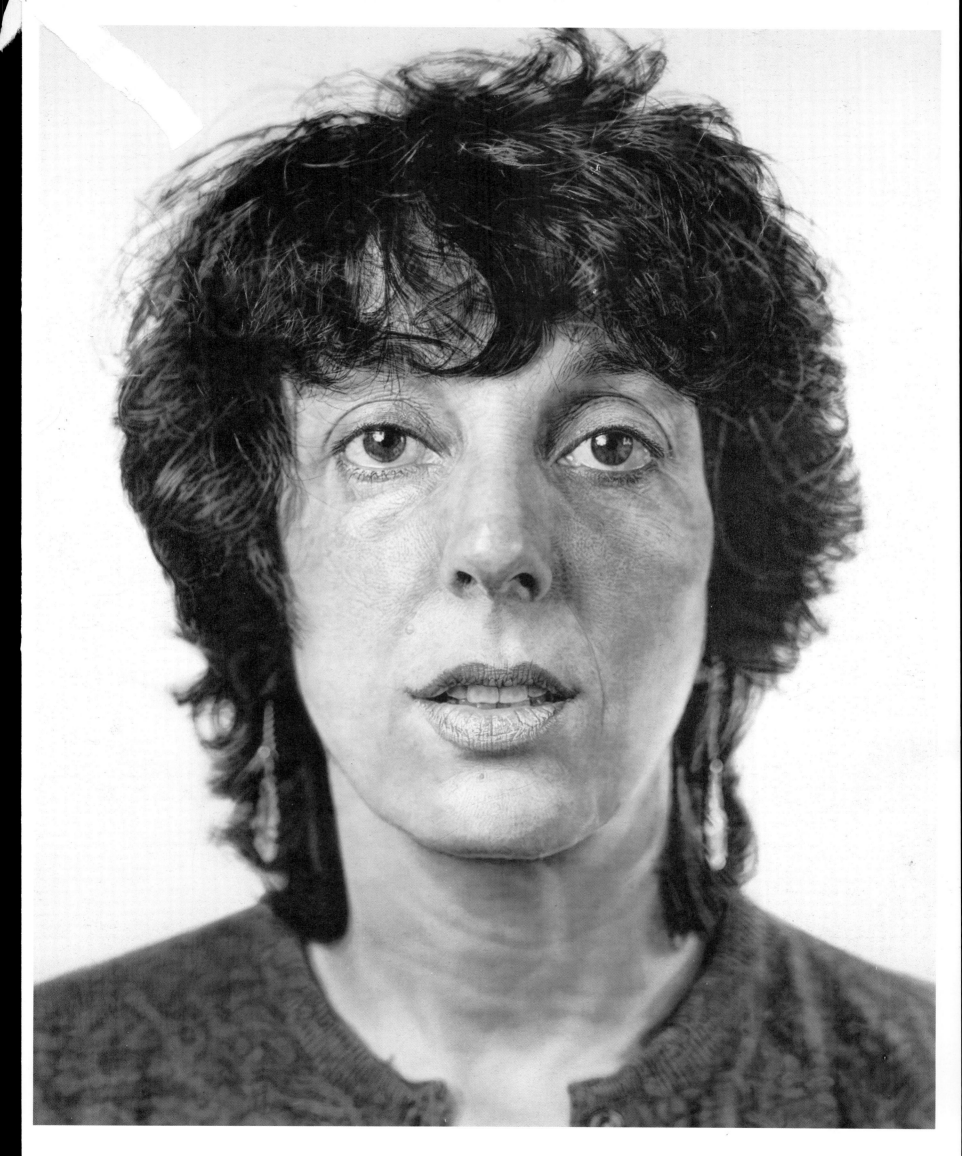

DICK (Fingerprint), 1981. Litho-ink on gray paper. Paper size, 29 × 21¾ in.
Mr. and Mrs. A. Barry Hirschfeld collection, Denver

GEORGIA (Fingerprint), 1981. Litho-ink on gray paper. Paper size, 29 × 22 in.
The Gelco collection, Eden Prairie, Minnesota

SELF-PORTRAIT, 1980
Charcoal on paper
Paper size, 43 × 30½ in.
Sidney Singer collection, Mamaroneck, New York

GEORGIA, 1980
Stamp-pad ink on paper
Paper size, 43 × 30½ in.
Barry and Gail Berkus collection, Santa Barbara, California

BEVAN, 1981. Litho-ink on paper. Paper size, 43 × 30¼ in.
AMA Art collection, Washington, D.C.

ARNE (second version), 1981. Litho-ink on paper. Paper size, 43 × 30½ in.
Art Institute of Chicago, Chicago

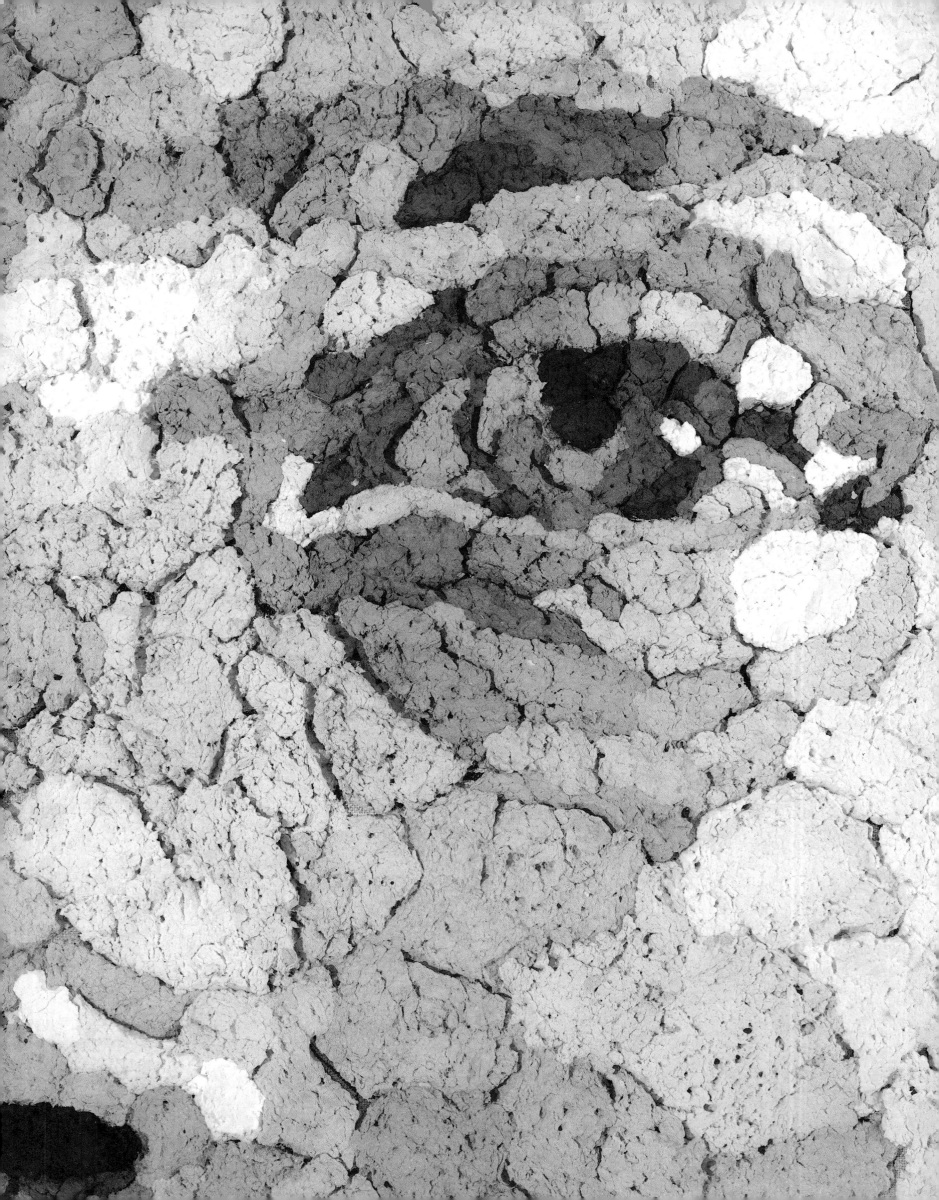

GEORGIA, 1985
Pulp paper on canvas
96 × 72 in.
The Pace Gallery, New York

GEORGIA, 1982
Pulp paper collage on canvas
48 × 38 in.
Collection of the artist

Opposite: Detail of **GEORGIA, 1985**

Left: At work on **JUD, 1982**

JUD, 1982. Pulp paper collage on canvas. 96 × 72 in. Gift of the Sydney and Frances Lewis collection, Virginia Museum of Fine Art, Richmond.

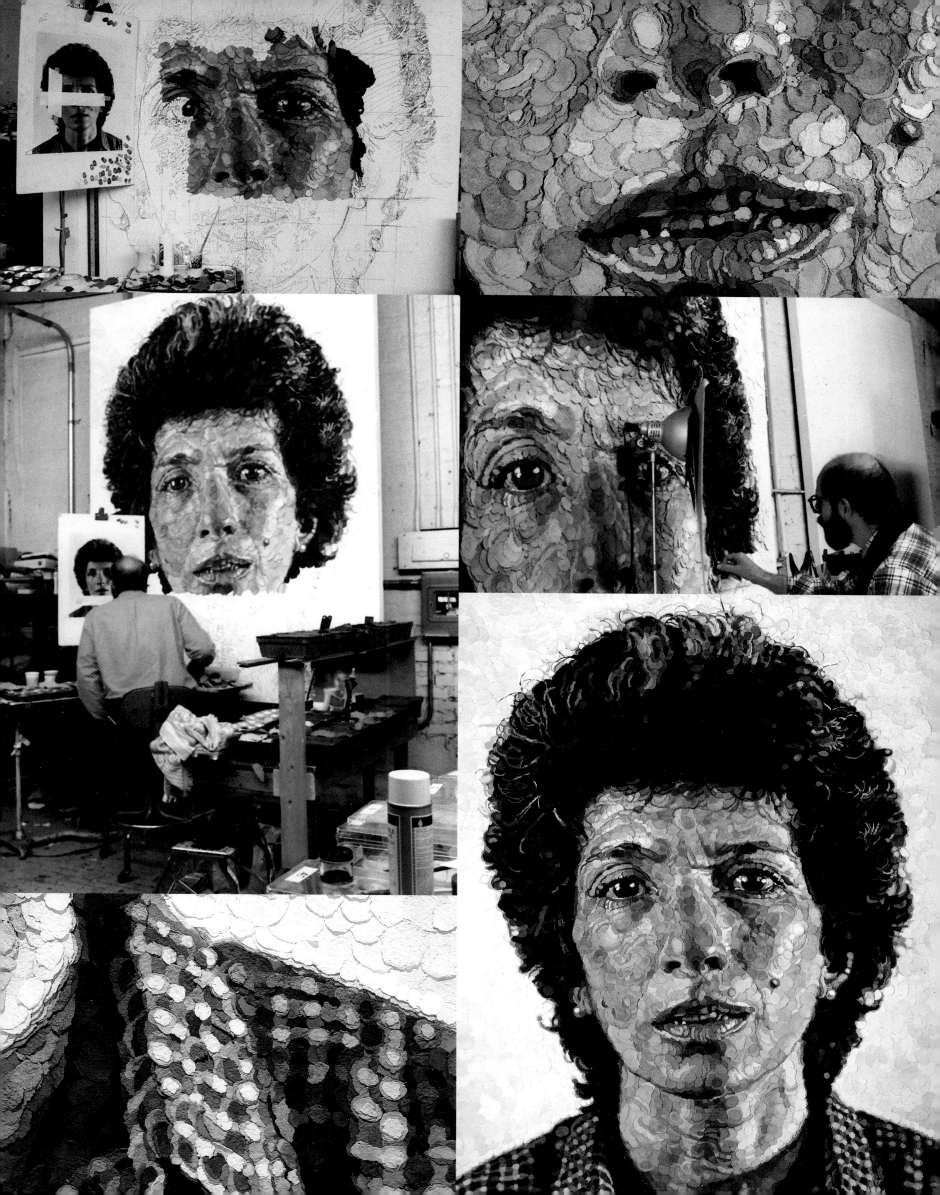

Preceding pages:
PHYLLIS, 1984, details and in progress
Pulp paper collage on canvas
96 × 72 in.
Equitable Life Assurance Company, New York

JOHN/FINGERPAINTING, 1984
Oil on canvas
24 × 20 in.
Diane and David Goldsmith collection, Orinda, California

MARK/PROGRESSION, 1983. Ink on paper. Paper size, 30 × 80 in. The Pace Gallery, New York

JOHN/PROGRESSION, 1983. Ink on paper. Paper size, 30 × 80 in. The Pace Gallery, New York

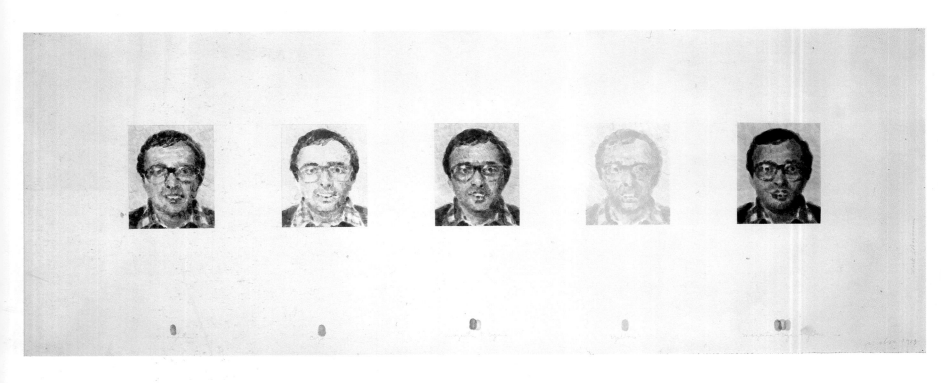

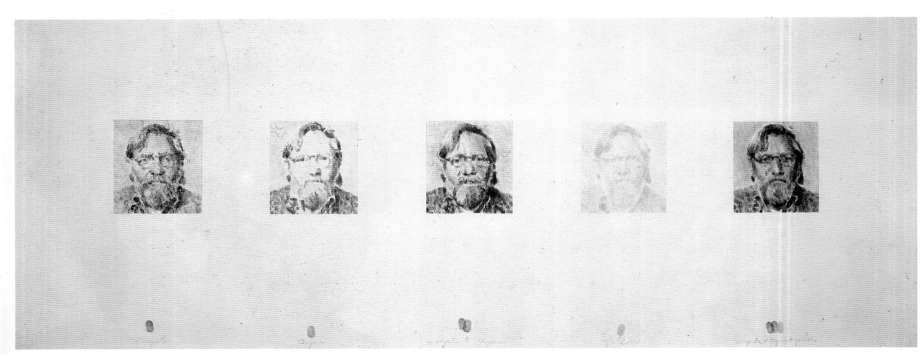

MARK/FINGERPRINT, 1984
Ink on paper
Paper size, 49 × 38 in.
Anne and Joel Ehrenkranz collection, New York

JOHN/FINGERPRINT, 1983
Ink on paper
Paper size, 48 × 38 in.
Edward L. Gardner, Larchmont, New York

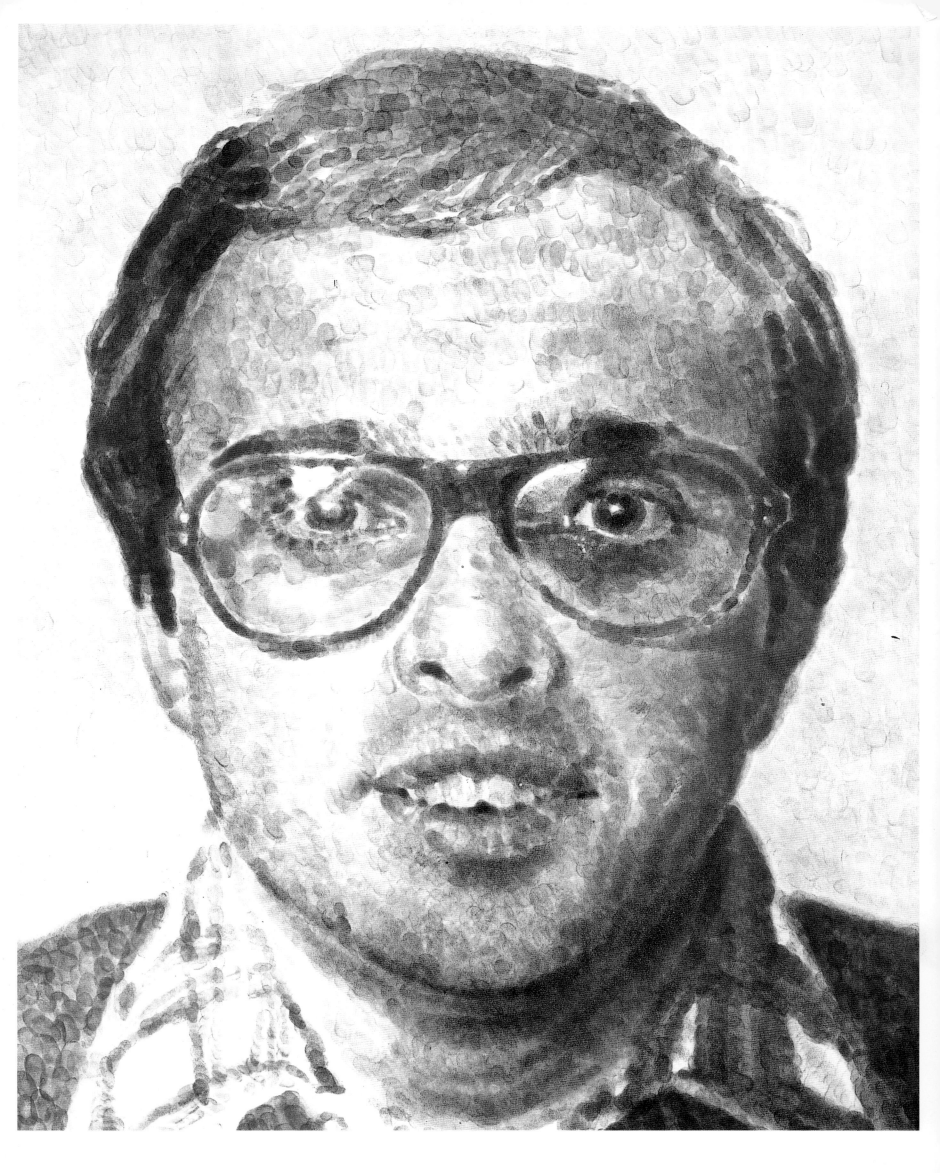

LESLIE/PASTEL, 1985
Pastel on watercolor-washed pulp paper
Paper size, 41 × 32 in.
Edward J. Minskoff collection, New York

Following pages:
At work on **LESLIE/FINGERPAINTING, 1985**

GEORGIA/FINGERPAINTING, 1984
Oil on canvas
48 × 38 in.
Fuji Television Gallery Company, Ltd., Tokyo, Japan

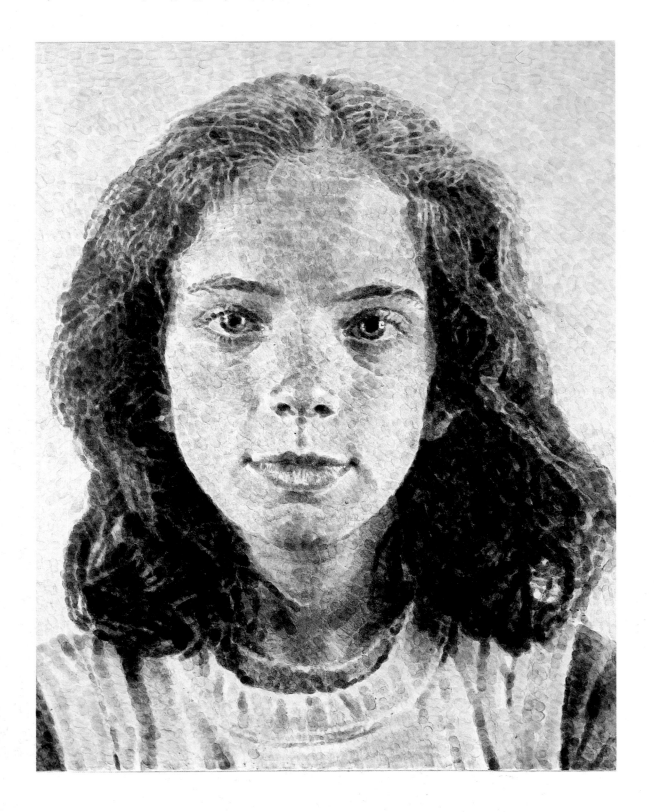

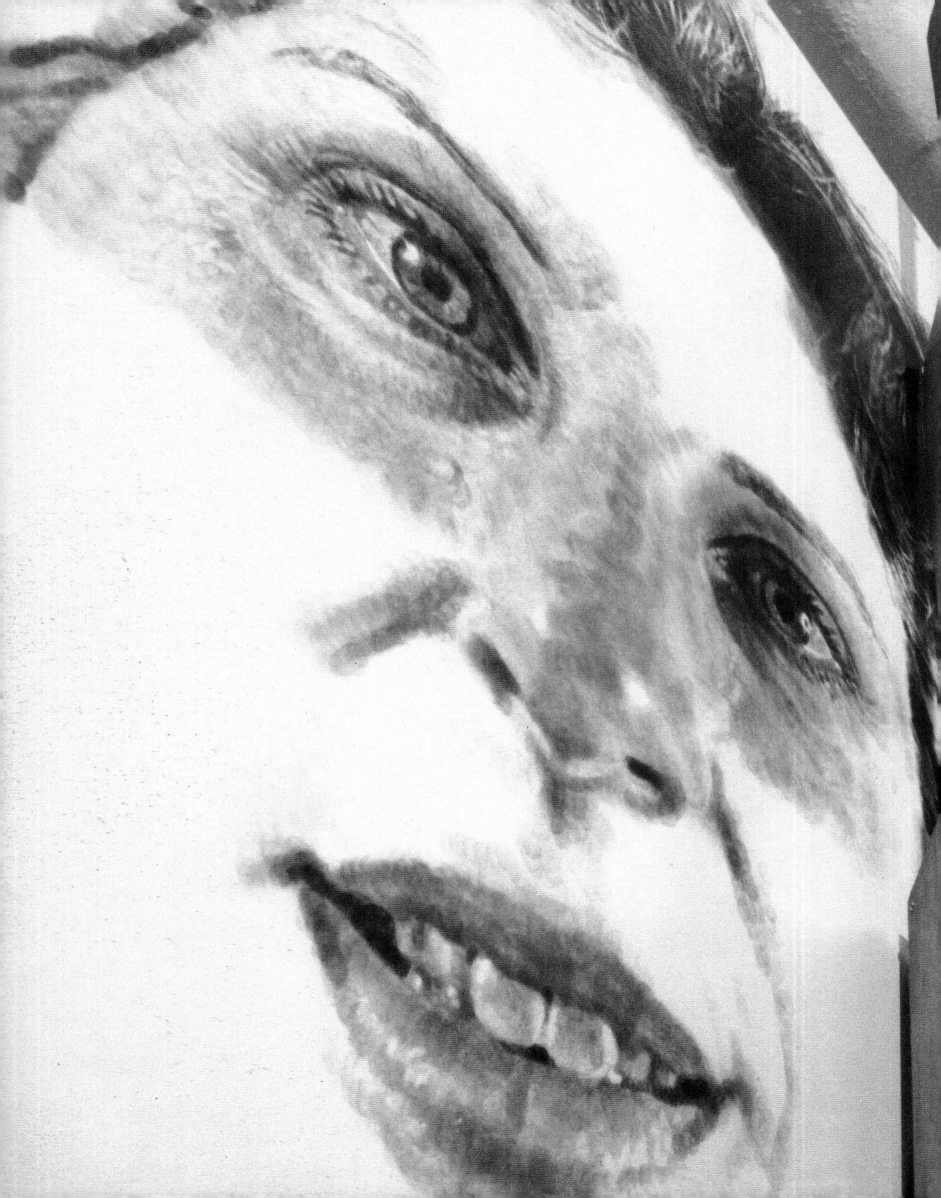

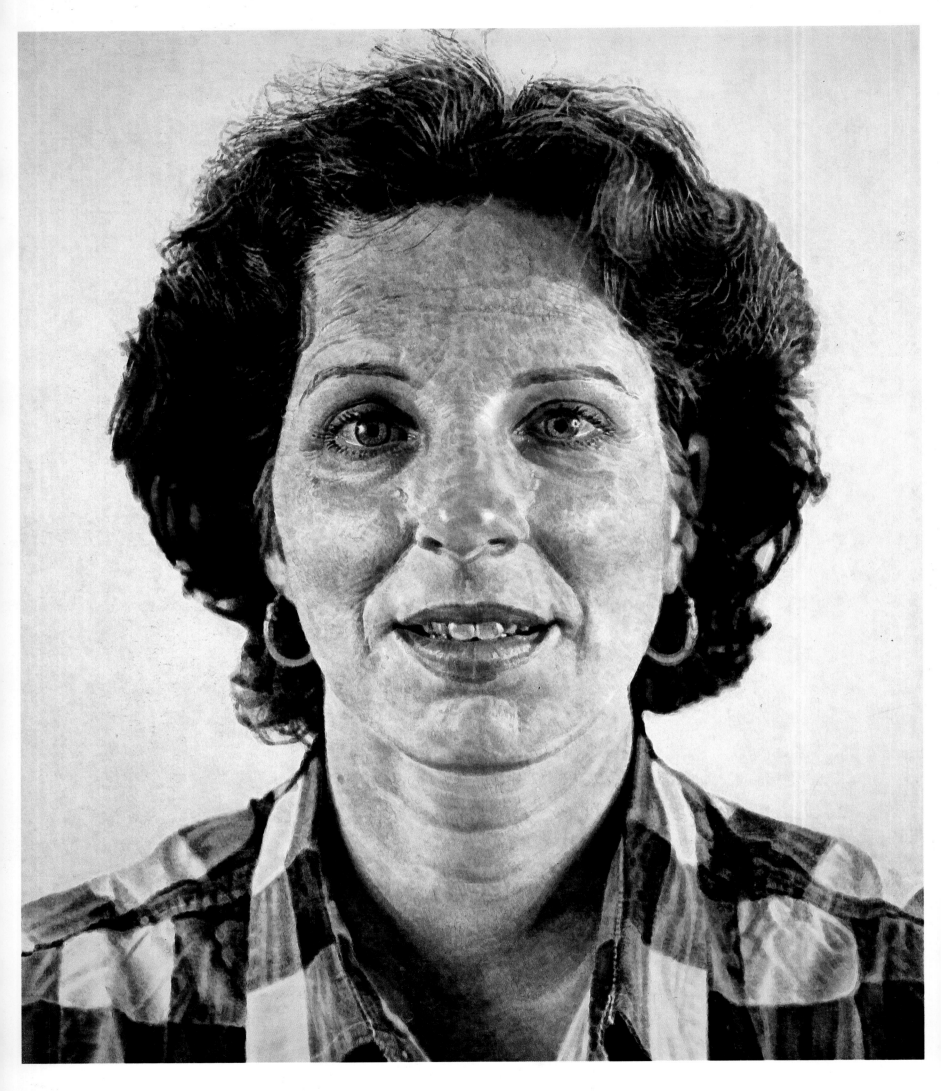

LESLIE/FINGERPAINTING, 1985
Oil-based ink on canvas
102 × 84 in.
Michael and Judy Ovitz collection, Los Angeles

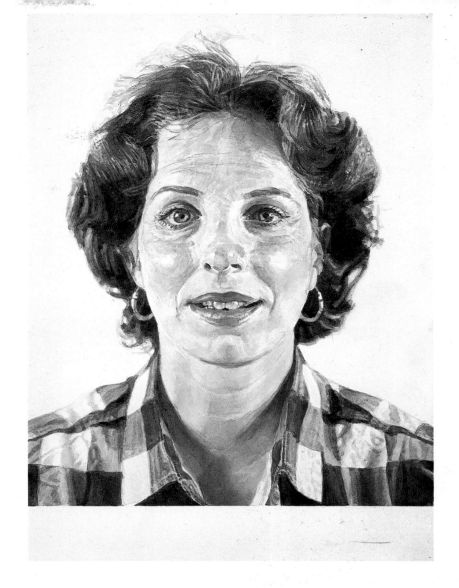

LESLIE/WATERCOLOR I, 1986
Watercolor on paper
Paper size, 30½ × 22¼ in.
The Pace Gallery, New York

LESLIE/WATERCOLOR II, 1986
Watercolor on paper
Paper size, 30½ × 22¼ in.
The Pace Gallery, New York

SELF-PORTRAIT, 1986. Oil on canvas. 54½ x 42¼ in.
David and Jeanine Smith collection, Pacific Palisades, California

Opposite: Details of **SELF-PORTRAIT, 1986**

FANNY/FINGERPAINTING, 1985. Oil on canvas. 102 × 84 in.
Lila Acheson Wallace Fund, National Gallery of Art, Washington, D.C.

Opposite: Detail of **FANNY/FINGERPAINTING, 1985**

GEORGIA/FINGERPAINTING, 1986
White oil-based ink on black acrylic-washed gessoed canvas
48 × 38 in.
The Pace Gallery, New York

MARTA/FINGERPAINTING, 1986
White oil-based ink on black acrylic-washed gessoed canvas
24 × 20 in.
The Pace Gallery, New York

Top, left to right:
FANNY, 1984
Litho-ink on silk paper
Paper size, 19 × 15½ in.
The Parrish Art Museum, Southhampton, New York

GEORGIA, 1984
Litho-ink on silk paper
Paper size, 19½ × 15½
Georgia Close collection, New York

MARTA, 1984
Litho-ink on silk paper
Paper size, 19 × 15¼ in.
Glenys and Kermit Birchfield collection, Atlanta, Georgia

Bottom, left to right:
MAGGIE, 1984
Litho-ink on silk paper
Paper size, 19⅛ × 15½ in.
Maggie Close collection, New York

SHIRLEY, 1984
Litho-ink on silk paper
Paper size, 19½ × 15½ in.
The Pace Gallery, New York

EMILY, 1984
Litho-ink on silk paper
Paper size, 19½ × 15½ in.
The Pace Gallery, New York

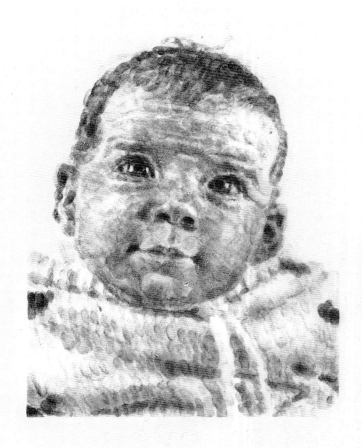

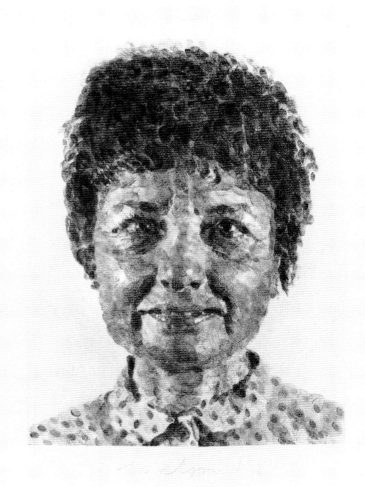

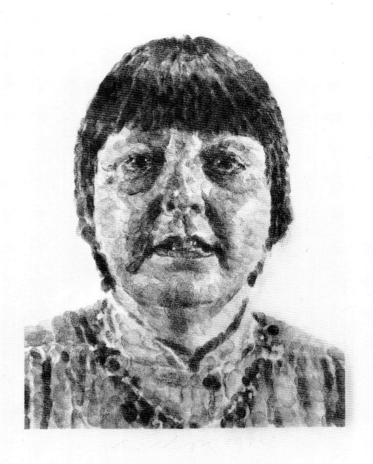

JANE, 1984
Litho-ink on silk paper
Paper size, 19½ × 15½ in.
The Pace Gallery, New York

LESLIE, 1984
Litho-ink on silk paper
19⅛ × 15 in.
Judith Harney collection, New York

PHOTOGRAPHS AND MULTIPLES

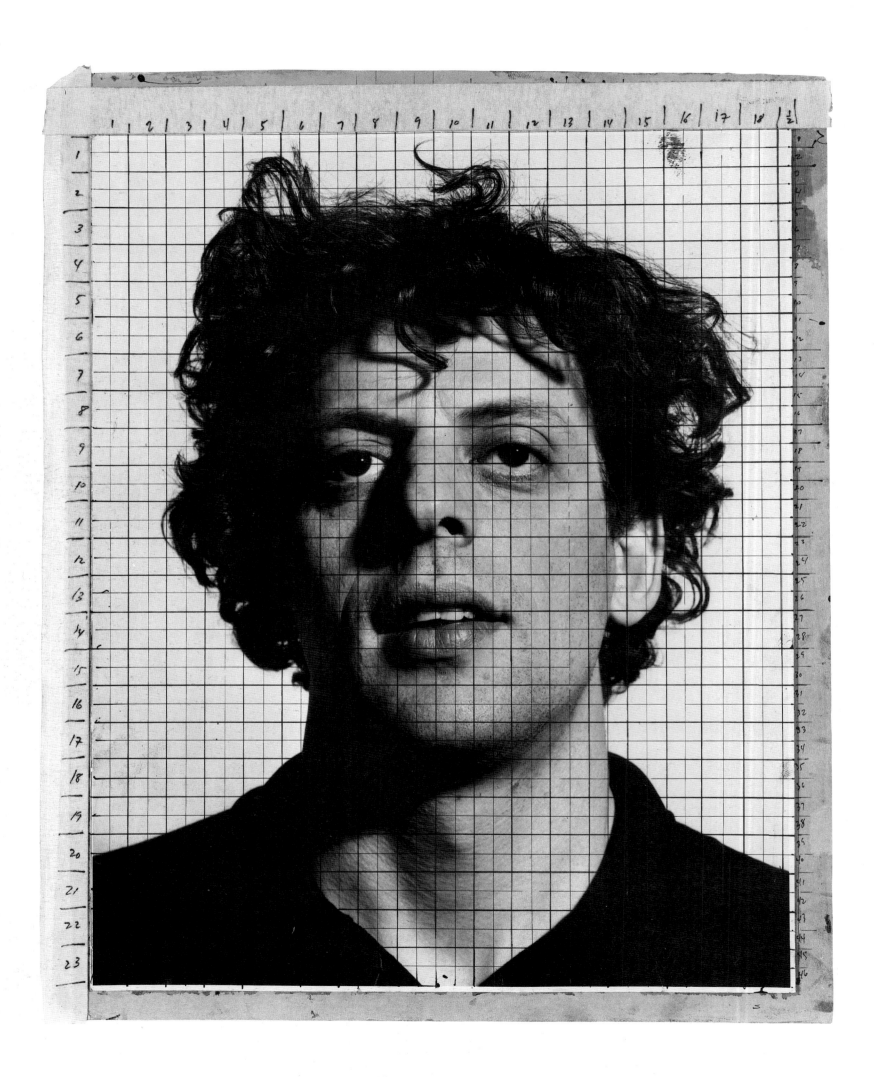

Working photograph for PHIL, 1969. Ink and masking tape on photograph mounted on cardboard
International Museum of Photography, George Eastman House, Rochester, New York

Following pages:
At work on, installation of, and details of **SELF-PORTRAIT/COMPOSITE/SIX PARTS, 1980**
Polaroid photographs. 170 × 133 in.
Collection of the artist

SELF-PORTRAIT/COMPOSITE/NINE PARTS, 1979. Polaroid photographs. 69 × 83 in.
Collection of the artist

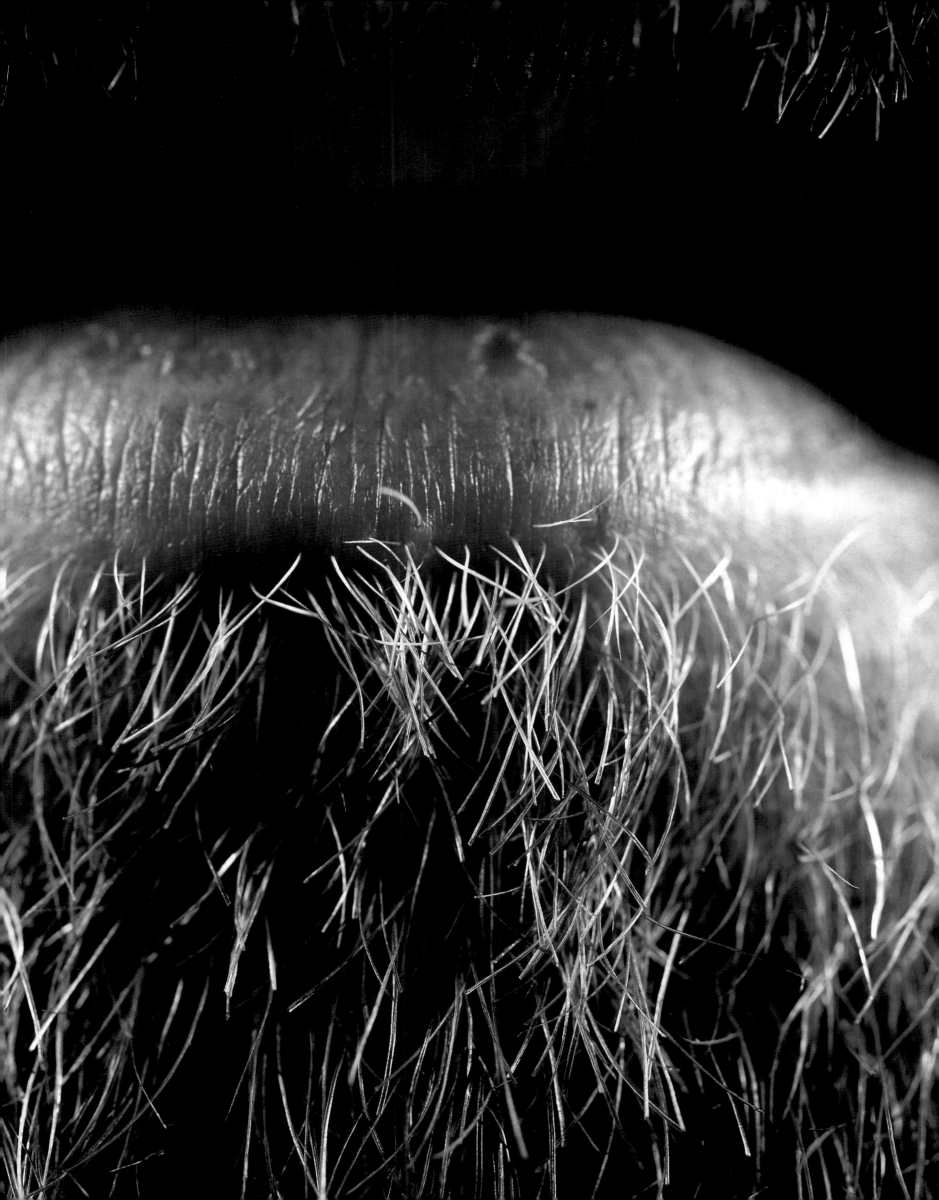

BERTRAND II

BERTRAND II, 1984
Polaroid photographs
85 × 208 in.
Collection of the artist

LAURA I, 1984, and the artist
Polaroid photographs
85 × 208 in.
Collection of the artist

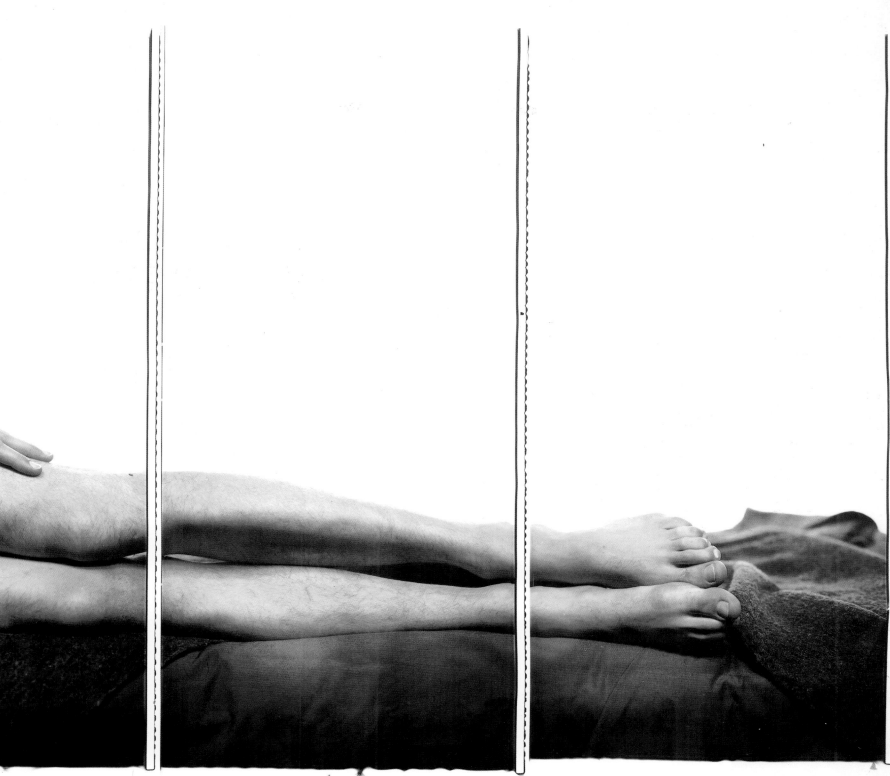

r. clon 1984

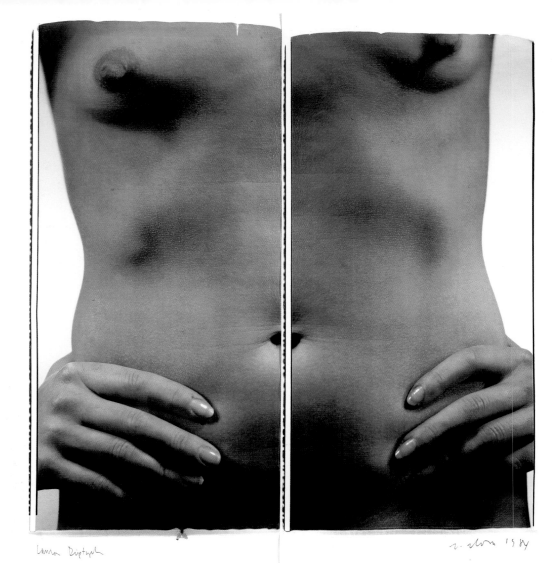

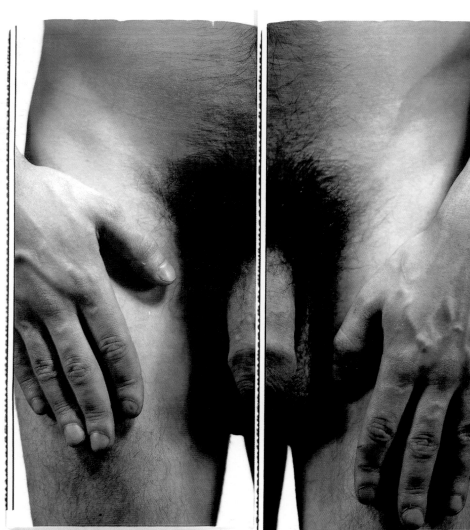

LAURA DIPTYCH, 1984
Polaroid photographs
Each panel, 40 × 80 in.
Collection of the artist

MARK DIPTYCH II, 1984
Polaroid photographs
Each panel, 40 × 80 in.
Collection of the artist

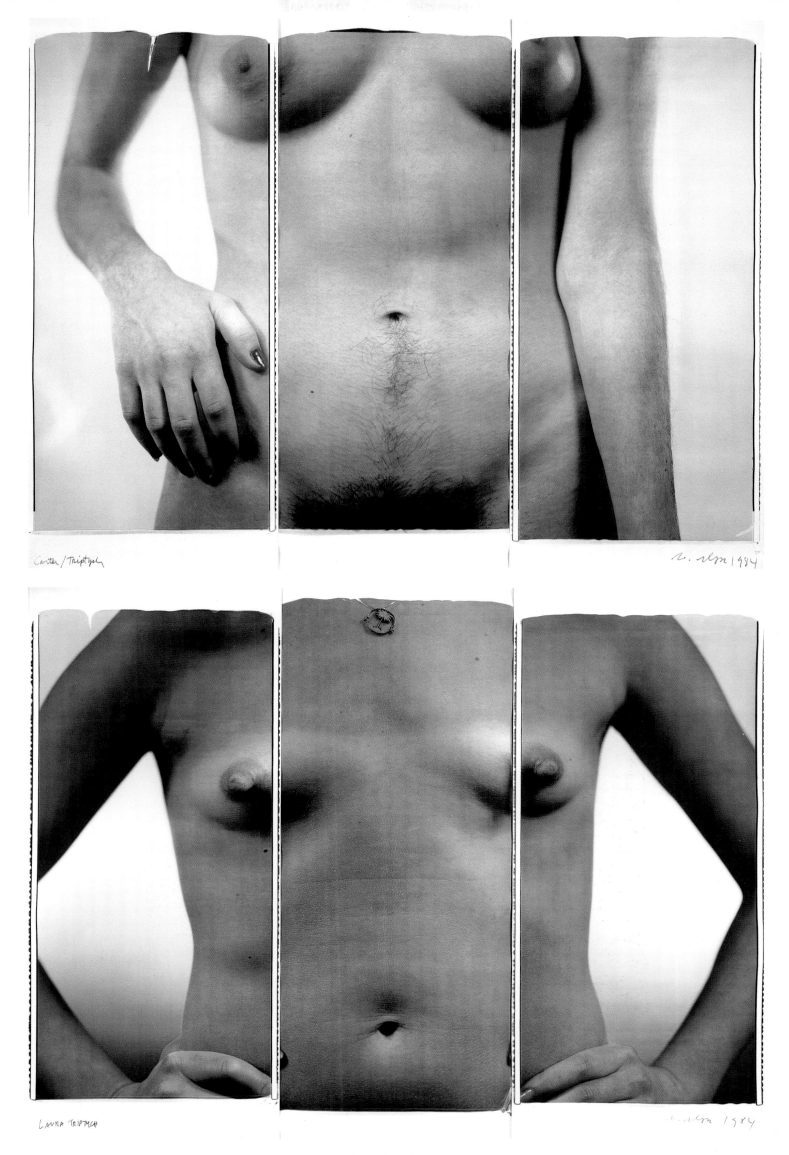

Top: **CARTER TRIPTYCH, 1984.** Polaroid photos. 85 × 128 in. Collection of the artist
Bottom: **LAURA TRIPTYCH, 1984.** Polaroid photos. 85 × 128 in. Collection of the artist

SELF-PORTRAIT/MANIPULATED, 1982
Handmade paper
Paper size, 38½ × 28½ in.
Edition: 25

ARNE, 1980
Polaroid photograph
84 × 44¾ in.
The Pace Gallery, New York

CARL, 1980
Polaroid photograph
84 × 44¾ in.
The Pace Gallery, New York

KEITH/MEZZOTINT, 1972. Mezzotint on paper. Paper size, 51½ × 42 in. Edition: 10

KEITH/MEZZOTINT, 1972, in progress

KEITH/FOUR TIMES, 1975. Lithograph. Paper size, 30½ × 88 in. Edition: 50

SELF-PORTRAIT, 1977. Etching. Paper size, 54 × 41 in. Edition: 35

SELF-PORTRAIT/WHITE INK VERSION, 1978. Etching and aquatint printed in white ink on black paper. Paper size, 54 × 40½ in. Edition: 35

PHIL I, II, III, 1982
Handmade paper, press dried
Each, paper size, 69 × 53½ in.
Each, Edition: 15
PHIL I on white paper
PHIL II on gray paper
PHIL III on black paper

KEITH I, II, III, 1981
Handmade paper, press dried
Each, paper size, 35 × 26¾ in.
Each, Edition: 20
KEITH I on gray paper
KEITH II on white paper
KEITH III on black paper

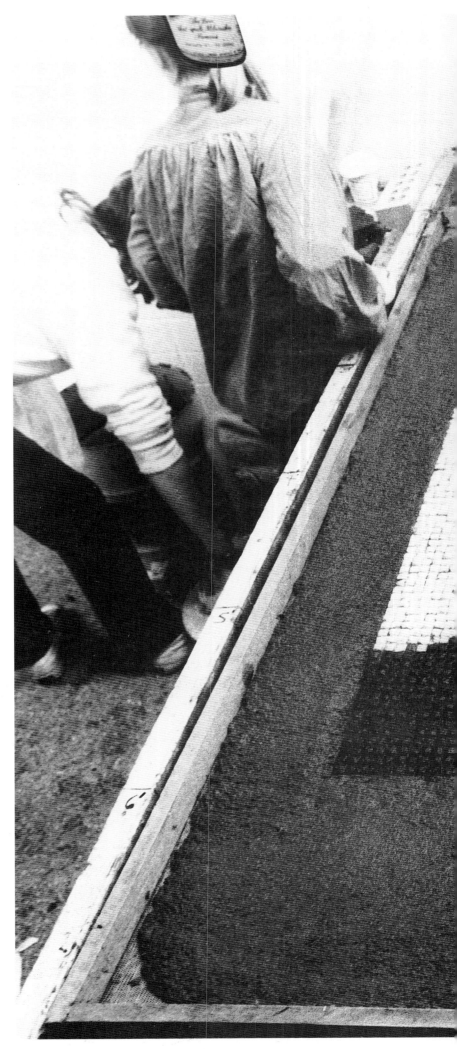

Papermaker Joe Wilfer at work on **PHIL**

GEORGIA, 1984. Handmade paper. Paper size, 56 × 44 in. Edition: 35

MARTA/FINGERPRINT, 1986. Etching. Paper size, 54 × 41 in. Edition: 45

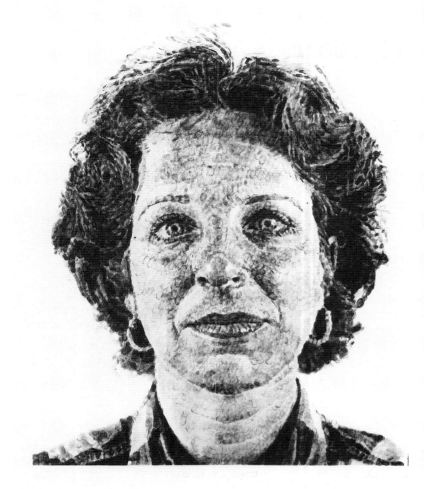

Above:
GEORGIA/FINGERPRINT, 1986
Etching
Paper size, 30 × 22½ in. Edition: 35

Above right:
LESLIE/FINGERPRINT, 1986
Etching
Paper size, 54 × 41 in. Edition: 45

Below right:
EMILY/FINGERPRINT, 1986
Etching
Paper size, 54 × 41 in. Edition: 45

EXHIBITION HISTORY

Exhibitions accompanied by an important catalogue
are indicated with an asterisk.

ONE-PERSON EXHIBITIONS

1967

Chuck Close, Art Gallery, University of Massachusetts, Amherst

1970

Chuck Close, Bykert Gallery, New York, 28 February–28 March

1971

Chuck Close: Recent Work, Los Angeles County Museum of Art, Los Angeles, 21 September–14 November

1971–72

Chuck Close: Recent Work, Bykert Gallery, New York. 4 December 1971–5 January 1972

1972

Chuck Close, Museum of Contemporary Art, Chicago, 19 March–May

1973

Chuck Close, The Akron Art Museum, Akron, Ohio

Chuck Close: Recent Work, Bykert Gallery, New York, 20 October–15 November

Chuck Close: Project, The Museum of Modern Art, New York

1975

Chuck Close, Bykert Gallery, New York

Chuck Close Prints, Edwin A. Ulrich Museum, Wichita State University, Wichita, Kansas; Mint Museum of Art, Charlotte, North Carolina; Ball State University Art Gallery, Muncie, Indiana; Phoenix Art Museum, Phoenix, Arizona; Minneapolis Institute of Art, Minneapolis

Chuck Close, The Portland Center for the Visual Arts, Portland, Oregon

1975–76

Chuck Close: Dot Drawings 1973–75, Laguna Gloria Art Museum, Austin, Texas, 17 June–20 July 1975; Texas Gallery, Houston, 22 July–16 August 1975; Art Museum of South Texas, Corpus Christi, 19 August–20 September 1975; San Francisco Museum of Modern Art, San Francisco; Contemporary Arts Center, Cincinnati

1976

Chuck Close, Baltimore Museum of Art, Baltimore

1977

Chuck Close: Recent Work, The Pace Gallery, New York, 30 April–4 June

1977–78

Chuck Close/Matrix 35, Wadsworth Atheneum, Hartford, Connecticut

1979

Chuck Close: Copie/Conforme?, Musée National d'Art Moderne, Centre National d'Art et de Culture Georges Pompidou, Paris

Chuck Close, Kunstraum München, Munich, 18 June–21 July

Chuck Close: Recent Work, The Pace Gallery, New York, 26 October–24 November

1980–81

Close Portraits, (A retrospective exhibition) The Walker Art Center, Minneapolis, September–October 1980. Traveled to Saint Louis Art Museum, St. Louis, December 1980–January 1981; Museum of Contemporary Art, Chicago, February–March 1981; The Whitney Museum of American Art, New York, April–June 1981

1982

Chuck Close: Photographs, California Museum of Photography, University of California, Riverside, June–July. Traveled to University Art Museum, University of California, Berkeley, 3 March–5 May

1982–83

Chuck Close: Paperworks, Richard Gray Gallery, Chicago, September–October 1982; John Stoller Gallery, Minneapolis, October–November 1982; Jacksonville Art Museum, Jacksonville, 10 December 1982–19 January 1983; Greenberg Gallery, St. Louis, September–October 1983

1983

Chuck Close: Recent Work, The Pace Gallery, New York, 25 February–26 March

1984–85

Chuck Close Paper Works, Herbert Palmer Gallery, Los Angeles, 4 February–March 1984. Traveled to Spokane Center of Art, Cheney, Washington, 5 April–12 May 1984; Milwaukee Art Museum, Milwaukee, 1 June–30 September 1984; N.I.U. Art Gallery, Northern Illinois University, DeKalb, 25 September–October 1984; Columbia Museum, Columbia, South Carolina, 18 November 1984–January 1985

1985

Chuck Close: Works on Paper, Contemporary Arts Museum, Houston, 8 March–31 April

Exhibition of Chuck Close, Fuji Television Gallery Company, Ltd., Tokyo, 1–30 March

Chuck Close: Photographs, Pace/MacGill Gallery, New York, 12 January–16 February

Chuck Close Large-Scale Photographs, Fraenkel Gallery, San Francisco, 26 June–27 July

1986

Chuck Close, Maquettes, Pace/MacGill Gallery, New York, 9 January–15 February

Chuck Close: Recent Work, The Pace Gallery, New York, 21 February–22 March

1987

Chuck Close Polaroids, Aldrich Museum of Contemporary Art, Ridgefield, Connecticut, 1 March–April

GROUP EXHIBITIONS

1969

Bykert Gallery, New York

Contemporary American Paintings (Biennial Exhibition), The Whitney Museum of American Art, New York

1970

Klischee und Antiklischee, Neue Galerie der Stadt, Aachen

Three Young Americans, Allen Memorial Art Museum, Oberlin College, Oberlin, Ohio

22 Realists, The Whitney Museum of American Art, New York

1971

Prospekt 71, Stadtische Kunsthalle, Düsseldorf

1972

Amerikanischer Fotorealismus, Wurtembergischer Kunstverein, Stuttgart

Art Around 1970, Neue Galerie der Stadt, Aachen

Colossal Scale, Sidney Janis Gallery, New York

Documenta 5, Kassel, West Germany

Eight New York Painters, Berkeley Museum, University of California, Berkeley

Eighteenth National Print Exhibition, Brooklyn Museum of Art, 22 November–4 February 1973. Traveled to California Palace of the Legion of Honor, 24 March–17 June 1973

Hyperréalistes Américains, Galerie des Quatre Mouvements, Paris, 25 October–25 November

Painting and Sculpture Today, 1972, Indianapolis Museum of Art, Indianapolis

Annual Exhibition, The Whitney Museum of American Art, New York

Realism Now, New York Cultural Center, New York, 6 December 1972–7 January 1973

1973

Aachen International 70–74, Edinburgh Festival, Royal Scottish Academy

American Art—Third Quarter Century, Seattle Art Museum, Seattle, 22 August–14 October

American Drawings 1963–1973, The Whitney Museum of American Art, New York

Amerikanischer Fotorealismus, Frankfurter Kunstverein, Frankfurt, West Germany. Traveled to Wuppertal Kunst und Museumsverein, Wuppertal, West Germany

Art Conceptuel et Hyperréaliste, Ludwig Collection, Musée d'Art Moderne de la Ville de Paris

Combattimento per un'immagine, Galleria Civica d'Arte Moderna, Turin, 4 March

Ein Grobes Jahrzehnt Amerikanischer Kunst, Ludwig Collection, Cologne/Aachen

Ekstrem Realisme, Louisiana Museum, Udgivet of Louisiana, Humleback, Denmark

Grands Maîtres Hyperréalistes Américains, Galerie des Quatre Mouvements, Paris

Hyperréalisme, Galerie Isy Brachot, Brussels

Kunst nach Wirklichkeit ein Neuer Realismus in Amerika und in Europe, Kunstverein Hanover, Hanover

Photo-Realism: The Ludwig Collection, Serpentine Gallery, London

Realism Now, Katonah Gallery, Katonah, New York

Ruhr Festival Exhibition, Recklinghausen, West Germany

The Emerging Real, Storm King Art Center, Mountainville, New York

The Super-Realist Vision, DeCordova and Dana Museum, Lincoln, Massachusetts, 7 October–9 December

Young American Artists. Traveled to Denmark, Norway, Sweden, and Germany

1974

Amerikaans Fotorealisme/Grafiek, Palais van Schone Kunsten, Brussels

ARS '74, Ateneum, The Fine Arts Academy of Finland, Helsinki, 15 February–31 March

Art 5 '74, Basel, 19–24 June

Hyperréalistes Américains/Réalistes Européens, Centre National d'Art Contemporain, Paris

Kijken naar de Werkelijkheid, Museum Boymans-van-Beuningen, Rotterdam, 1 June–18 August

New Portraits, The Whitney Museum of American Art, Downtown Branch, New York

Palazzo Reale, Milan

Projekts '74 (Kunst Bleibt Kunst), Wallraf-Richartz Museum, Cologne

Selections of Realistic Painting from the Ludwig Collection, Groninger Museum voor Stad en Lande, Groningen, The Netherlands

Three Realists: Close, Estes, Raffael, Worcester Art Museum, Worcester, Massachusetts, 27 February–7 April

11th Tokyo Biennale 1974, Tokyo

1975

Painting, Drawing, and Sculpture of the 60s and 70s from the Collection of Dorothy and Herbert Vogel, Institute of Contemporary Art, University of Pennsylvania, Philadelphia

Portrait Painting 1970–1975, Allan Frumkin Gallery, New York

Selections from the Collection of Herbert and Dorothy Vogel, Clocktower, New York

The Portrait/1975, Boston University Art Gallery, School for the Arts, December

34th Biennial Exhibition of Contemporary Painting, Corcoran Gallery of Art, Washington, D.C.

1975–76

Recent American Etching, Davison Art Center, Wesleyan University, Middletown, Connecticut, 10 October–23 November, 1975. Traveled to National Collection of Fine Arts, Smithsonian Institution, Washington, D.C., 21 January–27 March, 1976

1976

American Master Drawings and Watercolors, The Whitney Museum of American Art, New York

Modern Portraits: The Self and Others, Columbia University for Wildenstein & Company Gallery, New York

Seventy-second American Exhibition, Art Institute of Chicago

Soho, Akademie der Kunst, West Berlin

The Emerging Real, Storm King Art Center, Mountainville, New York

The Photographer and the Artist, Sidney Janis Gallery, New York

Three Decades of American Art Selected by the Whitney Museum of American Art, Seibu Museum of Art, Tokyo, 18 June–20 July

1976–77

American Artists: A New Decade, Fort Worth Art Museum. Traveled to Detroit Institute of Arts; Grand Rapids Arts Museum

Drawing Now, The Museum of Modern Art, New York. Traveled to College of Art, Edinburgh; Kunsthaus, Zurich; Kunsthalle, Baden-Baden, West Germany; Sonjia Henie-Niels Onstad Museum, Oslo

Drawings Today in New York, Tulane University, New Orleans. Traveled to Rice University, Houston; Southern Methodist University, Dallas; University of Texas at Austin; Oklahoma Art Center, Oklahoma City; and Dayton Art Institute, Dayton

Three-Person Exhibition: Richard Artschwager, Chuck Close, Joe Zucker, Daniel Weinberg Gallery, San Francisco. Traveled to La Jolla Museum of Contemporary Art; Memorial Union Art Gallery, University of California at Davis, California

1976–78

Aspects of Realism. Traveled to: Stratford, Ontario; Vancouver Centennial Museum; Glenbow Alberta Institute, Calgary, Alberta; Mendel Art Gallery, Saskatoon, Saskatchewan; Winnipeg Art Gallery, Manitoba; Edmonton Art Gallery, Alberta; Memorial University Art Gallery, St. John's, Newfoundland; Confederation Art Gallery, Charlottetown, Prince Edward Island; Musée d'Art Contemporain, Montreal, Quebec; Dalhousie University Art Gallery, Halifax, Nova Scotia; Windsor Art Gallery, Ontario; London Art Gallery and McIntosh Memorial Art Gallery, Ontario; Art Gallery of Hamilton, Ontario

1977

A View of the Decade, Museum of Contemporary Art, Chicago, 10 September–10 November

American Drawings 1927–1977, Minnesota Museum of Art, St. Paul, 6 September–29 October

Biennial Exhibition, The Whitney Museum of American Art, New York

Documenta 6, Kassel, West Germany

Illusion of Reality. Traveled to Australian National Gallery, Canberra; Western Australian Art Gallery, Perth; Queensland Art Gallery, Brisbane; Art Gallery of New South Wales, Sidney; Art Gallery of South Australia, Adelaide; National Gallery of Victoria, Melbourne; Tasmanian Museum and Art Gallery, Hobart

New Realism: Modern Art Form, Boise Gallery of Art, Boise, Idaho

New York Now, Amherst College, Massachusetts, 1977

Paris—New York, Musée National d'Art Moderne, Centre National d'Art et de Culture Georges Pompidou, Paris, September

Twentieth-Century American Art from Friends' Collections, The Whitney Museum of American Art, New York, September

Works on Paper, Galerie de Gestlo, Hamburg, West Germany, 27 May–July 10

1977–78

Critics' Choice. Traveled to Joe and Emily Lowe Art Gallery, Syracuse University, New York, 12 November–11 December 1977; Munson-Williams-Proctor Institute Museum of Art, Utica, New York, 1–30 January 1978

Representations of America (organized by Metropolitan Museum of Art, New York). Traveled to Ministry of Culture, Moscow; The Hermitage, Leningrad; Palace of Art, Minsk

Works from the Collection of Dorothy and Herbert Vogel, University of Michigan Museum of Art, 11 November 1977–January 1978

1978

Contemporary Drawing/NY, University Art Museum, University of California at Santa Barbara, 22 February–26 March

Eight Artists, Philadelphia Museum of Art, Philadelphia, 29 April–25 June

Point, Philadelphia College of Arts, Philadelphia, 18 November–15 December

20th Century American Drawings: Five Years of Acquisitions, The Whitney Museum of American Art, New York, 20 July–1 October

1978–79

American Painting of the 1970s, Albright-Knox Art Gallery, Buffalo, New York, December 1978–14 January 1979. Traveled to Newport Harbor Art Museum, Newport Beach, California, 3 February–18 March 1979

Late Twentieth-Century Art, The Sydney and Frances Lewis Foundation, Anderson Gallery, Virginia Commonwealth University, Richmond, 5 December 1978–8 January 1979

The Grid: Format & Image in 20th Century Art. The Pace Gallery, New York, 16 December 1978–20 January 1979. Traveled to Akron Art Museum, Akron, Ohio, 24 March–6 May 1979

The Mechanized Image (organized by Karen Amiel, Arts Council of Great Britain). Traveled to City Museum and Art Gallery, Portsmouth; Graves Art Gallery, Sheffield; Camden Arts Centre, London; Hatton Art Gallery, Newcastle; Aberdeen Art Gallery and Museum, Aberdeen

1979

America Now: Young America: Painters of the '70s (assembled by New Museum of the International Communication Agency). Traveled to eastern Europe, Budapest, Spring

Artists by Artists, The Whitney Museum of American Art, Downtown Branch, New York, 25 October–28 November

As We See Ourselves: Artists' Self-Portraits, Heckscher Museum, Huntington, New York, 22 June–5 August

Black and White Are Colors: Paintings of the 1950s–1970s, Galleries of the Claremont Colleges: Montgomery Art Gallery, Pomona College; Lang Art Gallery, Scripps College; 28 January–7 March

Documents, Drawings and Collages: Fifty American Works on Paper from the Collection of Mr. and Mrs. Stephen D. Paine. Traveled to Williams College Art Museum, Williamstown, Massachusetts; Toledo Museum of Art, Toledo; John and Mable Ringling Museum of Art, Sarasota; Fogg Art Museum, Harvard University, Cambridge, Massachusetts

Drawings About Drawings Today, Ackland Art Museum, University of North Carolina, Chapel Hill, North Carolina, 1 January–11 March

Images of the Self, Hampshire College Art Gallery, Hampshire, Massachusetts, 2 February–14 March

Realist Space, C. W. Post Art Gallery, Greenvale, New York, 19 October–14 December

The Altered Photograph (24 Walls—24 Curators), P.S. 1, Long Island City, New York, 22 April–10 June

The Decade in Review: Selections from the 1970s. The Whitney Museum of American Art, New York, 19 June–2 September

Biennial Exhibition, The Whitney Museum of American Art, New York, 14 February–1 April

20 × 24, Light Gallery, New York, 4–27 October

1979–80

Reflections of Realism. Albuquerque Museum, Albuquerque, New Mexico, 4 November 1979–27 January 1980

1980

American Figure Painting, The Chrysler Museum, Norfolk, Virginia, October

American Portraiture Drawings, National Portrait Gallery, Washington, D.C.

Aspects of the 70s: Directions in Realism, Danforth Museum, Framingham, Massachusetts, 17 May–24 August

First Person Singular: Recent Self Portraiture, Pratt Manhattan Center Gallery, 2 February–1 March; Pratt Institute Gallery, Brooklyn, New York, 5 March–1 April

Printed Art: A View of Two Decades, The Museum of Modern Art, New York

Self-Portraits: An Exhibition of Art on View at the Seagram Building, New York, 19 May–8 August

Ten American Artists from Pace, Wildenstein and Company, London, 18 June–18 July

The Figurative Tradition and The Whitney Museum of American Art: Paintings and Sculpture from the Permanent Collection, The Whitney Museum of American Art, New York, 25 June–28 September

The Morton G. Neumann Family Collection, The National Gallery of Art, Washington, D.C.

1980–81

American Painting of the Sixties and Seventies, Montgomery Museum of Fine Arts, Montgomery, Alabama, 4 April–25 May 1980. Traveled to: Joslyn Art Museum, Omaha, Nebraska, 1980; Museum of Fine Arts, St. Petersburg, Florida, 1980; Columbus Museum of Art, Columbus, Ohio, 1981; Colorado Springs Fine Art Center, Colorado Springs, Colorado, 1981; Sierra Nevada Museum of Art, Reno, Nevada, 1981

1981

Contemporary American Realism Since 1960, The Pennsylvania Academy of Fine Arts, Philadelphia, Pennsylvania, 18 September–13 December

Drawings from Georgia Collections: 19th and 20th Century, The High Museum of Art, Atlanta, 14 May–28 June

Seven Photorealists from New York Collections, The Solomon R. Guggenheim Museum, New York, 6 October–8 November

The Akron Art Museum, Akron, Ohio

20 Artists: Yale School of Art 1950–1970, Yale University Art Gallery, New Haven, Connecticut, 29 January–29 March

1981–82

American Prints: Process and Proofs, The Whitney Museum of American Art, New York, 25 November 1981–24 January 1982

Inside/Out, Self Beyond Likeness, Sullivan Gallery, Newport Harbor Art Museum, Newport Beach, California, 22 May–12 July 1981. Traveled to Portland Art Museum, Oregon, 8 September–18 October 1981; Joslyn Art Museum, Omaha, Nebraska, 13 February–April 1982

Instant Photography, Stedelijk Museum, Amsterdam, 4 December 1981–17 January 1982

Photographer as Printmaker: 140 Years of Photographic Printmaking (organized by The Arts Council of Great Britain). Traveled to: Ferens Art Gallery, Hull, 5–30 August 1981; The Cooper Gallery, Barnsley, 19 December 1981–17 January 1982; Castle Museum, Nottingham, 30 January–28 February 1982; The Photographer's Gallery, London, 11 March–11 April 1982

Super Realism from the Morton G. Neumann Family Collection, Kalamazoo Institute of the Arts, Michigan, 1 September–1 November, 1981. Traveled to The Art Center, Inc., South Bend, Indiana, 22 November 1981–3 January 1982; Springfield Art Museum, Springfield, Missouri, 16 January–28 February 1982; Dartmouth College Museum and Galleries, Hanover, New Hampshire, 19 March–2 May 1982; DeCordova and Dana Museum, Lincoln, Massachusetts, 9 May–20 June 1982; Des Moines Art Center, Des Moines, 6 July–15 August 1982

1981–83

Contemporary American Realism Since 1960, Pennsylvania Academy of Fine Arts, Philadelphia, 18 September–13 December 1981. Traveled to Virginia Museum, Richmond, 8 February–4 April 1982; Oakland Museum, Oakland, California, 6 May–25 July 1982; Germany and The Netherlands, Fall 1982; Gulbenkian Foundation, Lisbon, 10 September–24 October 1982; Salas de Exposiciónes de Belles Artes, Madrid, 17 November–27 December 1982; Kunsthalle, Nuremberg, 11 February–10 April 1983

1982

Great Big Drawings, Hayden Gallery, Massachusetts Institute of Technology, Cambridge, Massachusetts, 3 April–2 May

Homo Sapiens: The Many Images, The Aldrich Museum of Contemporary Art, Ridgefield, Connecticut, May

Surveying the Seventies, The Whitney Museum of American Art, Fairfield County Branch, 12 February–31 March

Late 20th Century Art, Worcester Art Museum, Worcester, Massachusetts, 10 September–31 October

Making Paper, American Craft Museum, New York, 20 May–26 September

Momentbild: Kunstlerphotographie, Kestner-Gessellschaft, Hanover, 5 March–18 April

New American Graphics 2: An Exhibition of Contemporary American Prints, Madison Art Center, University of Wisconsin, 13 March–25 April

Photo-Réalisme—Dix Ans Après, Galerie Isy Brachot, Paris, 13 January–6 March

The Human Figure, Contemporary Arts Center, New Orleans, 5 March–4 April

1982–83

Black & White, Leo Castelli Gallery, New York, 29 December 1982–9 February 1983

New Portraits: Behind Faces, Dayton Art Institute, Dayton, Ohio, 19 October 1982–6 February 1983

1983

American Super-Realism from the Morton G. Neumann Family Collection, Terra Museum of American Art, Evanston, Illinois, 4 November–7 December

Faces Since the 50s: A Generation of American Portraiture, Center Gallery, Bucknell University, Lewisburg, Pennsylvania, 11 March–17 April

New Work, New York, Newcastle Polytechnic Gallery, Newcastle-upon-Tyne, England, 8 October–4 November. Traveled to Harrowgate Gallery, Harrowgate, England

Photographic Visions by Martha Alf, Chuck Close, Robert Cumming, David Hockney, Robert Rauschenberg, Ed Ruscha, Los Angeles Center for Photographic Studies, Los Angeles, 10 September–16 October

Self-Portraits, Linda Farris Gallery, Seattle, 4 August–11 September. Traveled to Los Angeles Municipal Art Gallery, Los Angeles, 18 October–13 November

Subjective Vision, The Lucinda Bunnen Collection of Photographs, High Museum of Art, Atlanta

1984

Drawings by Contemporary American Figurative Artists, Maryland Institute, College of Art, Baltimore. 26 September–4 November

Drawings 1974–1984, Hirshhorn Museum and Sculpture Garden, Washington, D.C., 15 March–13 May

Paper Transformed: A National Exhibition of Paper Art, Turman Gallery, Indiana State University, Terre Haute

The First Show: Painting and Sculpture, Eight Collections, 1940–1980, Museum of Contemporary Art, Los Angeles

The Modern Art of The Print: Selections from the Collection of Lois and Michael Torf, Williams College Art Museum, Williamstown, Massachusetts, 5 May–16 July; Museum of Fine Arts, Boston, 1 August–14 October

The New Portrait, The Institute for Art and Urban Resources (P.S.1), Long Island City, New York, 15 April–10 June

1985

Daniel Weinberg Gallery, Los Angeles, 9–30 November

Workshop Experiments: Clay, Paper, Fabric, Glass, Brattleboro Museum and Art Center, Vermont, 18 October–8 December

American Realism: The Precise Image, Isetan Museum of Art, Tokyo. Traveled to Daimaru Museum, Osaka, Yokohama Takashimaya, 7 November–12 December

1985–86

Self-Portrait: The Photographers' Persona, 1840–1985, The Museum of Modern Art, New York, 7 November 1985–7 January 1986

1986

Nude Naked Stripped, Hayden Gallery, Massachusetts Institute of Technology, Cambridge, Massachusetts, 13 December 1985–2 February 1986

The Real Big Picture, The Queens Museum, New York, 17 January–19 March

50 Years Modern Color Photography, Cologne, Germany, 3–9 September

Painting and Sculpture Today—1986, Indianapolis Museum of Art, Indianapolis, Indiana, 24 June–24 August

Big and Small, Israel Museum, Jerusalem, Summer

The Changing Likeness: Twentieth-Century Portrait Drawings, The Whitney Museum of American Art at Philip Morris, New York, 27 June–4 September

Philadelphia Collects Art Since 1940, Philadelphia Museum of Art, Philadelphia, September–November

An American Renaissance: Painting and Sculpture Since 1940, Museum of Art, Fort Lauderdale, Florida, 12 January–30 March

Public and Private: American Prints Today, The 24th National Print Exhibition, The Brooklyn Museum of Art, New York, 7 February–5 May

Group Portrait Show, Martina Hamilton Gallery, New York, 21 April–3 June

70s into 80s, Museum of Fine Arts, Boston

1987

The Monumental Image, Sonoma University, Sonoma California

BIBLIOGRAPHY

BOOKS

Adrian, Dennis. *Sight Out of Mind: Essays and Criticism on Art*. Ann Arbor: UMI Research Press, 1985.

Alloway, Lawrence. *Great Drawings of All Time: The Twentieth Century*. (2 vols.) New York: Shorewood Fine Books, 1979.

Armstrong, Tom. *Amerikanische Malerei 1930–1980*. Munich: Prestel-Verlag, 1981.

Arnason, H. H. *History of Modern Art: Painting, Sculpture, Architecture*. 3d ed. New York: Harry N. Abrams, Inc., 1986.

Arthur, John. *Realist Drawings and Watercolors: Contemporary Works on Paper*. Boston: New York Graphic Arts Society/Little, Brown and Co., 1980.

———. *Realists at Work*. New York: Watson-Guptill Publications, 1983.

Ashton, Dore, and John Wilmerding, eds. *The Genius of American Painting*. New York: William Morrow and Co., 1973.

Baigell, Matthew. *A Concise History of American Painting and Sculpture*. New York: Harper and Row, 1984.

Battcock, Gregory, ed. *Super Realism: A Critical Anthology*. New York: E. P. Dutton, 1975.

Betti, Claudia, and Teel Sale. *Drawing: A Contemporary Approach*. New York: Holt, Rinehart and Winston, with Capital City Press, Vermont, 1980.

Bevlin, Marjorie E. *Design through Discovery*. 3d ed. New York: Holt, Rinehart and Winston, 1977.

Billeter, Erika. *Das Selbstportrait*. Lausanne: Musée Cantonal des Beaux-Arts, 1985; Bern: Benteli Verlag, 1985.

———. *Malerei und Photographie im Dialog*. Bern: Benteli Verlag, 1977.

Brachot, Isy, ed. *Hyperréalisme*. Brussels: Imprimeries F. Van Buggenhoudt, 1973.

Brommer, Gerald F., *Discovering Art History*. Worcester, Mass.: Davis Publications, Inc., 1981.

———, and George Horn. *Art in Your World*. Worcester, Mass.: Davis Publications, Inc., 1977.

Brown, Milton W., et al. *American Art: Painting, Sculpture, Architecture, Decorative Arts, Photography*. New York: Harry N. Abrams, Inc., 1979.

Bujese, Arlene, ed. *Twenty-five Artists*. Foreword by Thomas M. Messer. Frederick, Maryland: University Publications of America, Inc., 1982

Calamandrei, Mauro, with photographs by Gianfranco Gorgoni. *ART USA*. Milan: Fratelli Fabbri Editori, 1974.

Canaday, John. *What is Art? An Introduction to Painting, Sculpture, and Architecture*. New York: Alfred A. Knopf, 1980.

Castleman, Riva. *Prints of the 20th Century: A History*. New York: Holt, Rinehart and Winston, 1979.

Chase, Linda. *Hyperrealism*. Rev. ed. Paris: Filipacchi, 1973.

Coke, Van Deren. *The Painter and the Photograph: From Delacroix to Warhol*. Albuquerque: University of New Mexico Press, 1972.

Cotler, Sheldon, ed. *Photography Year/1974 Edition*. New York: Time-Life Books, 1974.

Cummings, Paul. *Twentieth-Century Drawings: Selections from the Whitney Museum of American Art*. New York: Dover Publications, 1981.

Daval, Jean-Luc. *Art Actuel/Skira Annuel 75*. Geneva: Skira, 1975.

———. *Art Actuel/Skira Annuel 78*. Geneva: Skira, 1978.

———. *Art Actuel/Skira Annuel 80*. Geneva: Skira, 1980.

———. *Photography: History of an Art*. New York: Rizzoli International Publications, 1982.

Dempsey, Michael. *The Year's Art 1969–70: Europe and the U.S.A.*. New York: G. P. Putnam's Sons, 1971.

Diamonstein, Barbaralee. *Inside New York's Art World*. New York: Rizzoli International Publications, 1979.

Distel, Herbert. *The Museum of Drawers*. Zurich: Kunsthaus Zurich, 1978.

Elsen, Albert E. *Purposes of Art*. 4th ed. New York: Holt, Rinehart and Winston, Inc., 1981.

Emanuel, Muriel, et al., eds. *Contemporary Artists*. 2d ed. New York: St. Martin's Press, 1983.

Feldman, Edmund Burke. *Thinking about Art*. Englewood Cliffs, N.J.: Prentice Hall Inc., 1985.

Finch, Christopher. *American Watercolors*. New York: Abbeville Press, 1986.

Fischl, Eric, and Jerry Saltz, eds. *Sketchbook with Voices*. New York: Alfred Van der Marck Editions, 1986.

Gabay, Neil. *Modern Painters*. Akron, Ohio: Nina Books, 1981.

Goldstein, Nathan. *One Hundred American and European Drawings: A Portfolio*. Englewood Cliffs, N.J.: Prentice Hall, 1982.

Goodrum, Charles A. *Treasures of the Library of Congress*. New York: Harry N. Abrams, Inc. 1980.

Goodyear, Frank H., Jr. *Contemporary American Realism Since 1960*. New York: New York Graphic Society, 1981.

Gorgoni, Gianfranco. *Beyond the Canvas: Artists of the Seventies and Eighties*. New York: Rizzoli International Publications, 1985.

Hertz, Richard. *Theories of Contemporary Art*. Englewood Cliffs, N.J.: Prentice Hall, 1985.

Hills, Patricia, and Tarbell, Roberta K. *The Figurative Tradition and the Whitney Museum of American Art*. New York: The Whitney Museum of American Art in association with University of Delaware Press, 1980.

Hunter, Sam, and John Jacobus. *Modern Art: Painting, Sculpture, Architecture*. 2d ed. New York: Harry N. Abrams, Inc., 1985.

Huyghe, Rene, ed. *Larousse Encyclopedia of Modern Art from 1880 to the Present Day*. New York: Excalibur Books, 1981.

Johnson, Ellen H., ed. *American Prints and Printmakers*. New York: Doubleday and Co., 1980.

Kaplan, Ellen. *Prints: A Collector's Guide*. New York: Coward-McCann, Inc., 1983.

Kramer, Hilton. *The Revenge of the Philistines: Art and Culture, 1972–1984*. New York: The Free Press, 1985.

Lee, Marshall. *Art at Work*. New York: E. P. Dutton, 1984.

Lindey, Christine. *Superrealist Painting and Sculpture*. New York: William Morrow and Co., 1980.

Lucie-Smith, Edward. *Art in the Seventies*. Ithaca, New York: Cornell University Press, 1980.

———. *Movements in Art Since 1945*. Rev. ed. New York: Thames and Hudson, 1985.

———. *Super Realism*. New York: E. P. Dutton, 1979.

Markowski, Eugene, D. *Image and Illusion*. Englewood Cliffs, N.J.: Prentice Hall, 1984.

Marshall, Richard, and Robert Mapplethorpe. *50 New York Artists*. San Francisco: Chronicle Books, 1986.

Martin, Alvin. *American Realism: Twentieth Century Drawings and Watercolors*. New York: Harry N. Abrams, Inc., in association with the San Francisco Museum of Art, 1986.

Meisel, Louis K. *Photorealism*. New York: Harry N. Abrams, Inc., 1980.

Melot, Michel, Antony Griffiths, and Richard S. Field. *Prints: History of an Art*. New York: Rizzoli International Publications, 1981.

Mendelowitz, Daniel. *Mendelowitz's Guide to Drawing*. Revised by Duane A. Wakeham. 3d ed. New York: CBS College Publishing/Holt, Rinehart and Winston, 1982.

Mollison, James, and Laura Murray, eds. *Australian National Gallery: An Introduction*. Canberra: Australian National Gallery, 1982.

Naylor, Colin, and Genesis P. Orridge. *Contemporary Artists*. Calne, England: Hilmarton Manor Press, 1978.

Oldenburg, Richard E. *The Museum of Modern Art: The History of the Collection*. New York: Harry N. Abrams, Inc., 1984.

Pelfrey, Robert, and Mary Hall-Pelfrey. *Art and Mass Media*. New York: Harper and Row, 1985.

Piper, David. *The Illustrated Library of Art*. 4 vols. New York: Portland House, 1986.

———, ed. *Looking at Art*. New York: Random House, 1984.

Popper, Frank. *Art—Action and Participation*. New York: New York University Press, 1975.

Rattemeyer, Volker. *Kunst und Median: Materialien zur Documenta 6*. Kassel, West Germany: Stadtzeitung Verlag, 1977.

Robins, Corinne. *The Pluralist Era: American Arts, 1968–1981*. New York: Harper and Row, 1984.

Robinson, Franklin W. *One Hundred Master Drawings from New England Private Collections*. Hanover, New Hampshire: The University Press of New England, 1973.

Rose, Barbara. *American Art Since 1900*. New York: Praeger Publishers, 1972.

———, ed. *Readings in American Art: 1900–1975*. Rev. ed. New York: Praeger Publishers, 1975.

Rosenblum, Naomi. *A World History of Photography*. New York: Abbeville Press, 1984.

Sachs, Samuel. *Favorite Paintings from the Minneapolis Institute of Arts*. New York: Abbeville Press, 1981.

Saff, Donald, and Deli Sacilotto. *Printmaking: History and Process*. New York: Holt, Rinehart and Winston, 1978.

Sager, Peter. *Neue Formen des Realismus*. Cologne: Verlag M. DuMont Schauberg, 1973.

Sellback, Jack. *Faces*. Worcester, Massachusetts: Davis Publications, 1977.

Selz, Peter. *Art in Our Times: A Pictorial History 1890–1980*. New York: Harry N. Abrams, Inc., 1981.

Sims, Patterson. Foreword by Tom Armstrong. *The Whitney Museum of American Art: Selected Works from the Permanent Collection*. New York: W. W. Norton in association with The Whitney Museum of American Art, 1985.

Stebbins, Theodore E., Jr. *American Master Drawings and Watercolors: A History of Works on Paper from Colonial Times to the Present*. New York: Harper and Row, 1976.

Thomas, Karin. *Bis Haute: Stilgeschichte der bildenen Kunste im 20 Jahrhundert*. Cologne: Verlag M. DuMont Schauberg, 1971.

Thomas, Karin, and Gerd de Vries. *DuMont's Kunstler Lexikon: Von 1945 bis zur Gegenwart*. Cologne: DuMont Buchverlag, 1977.

Vaizey, Marina. *The Artist As Photographer*. New York: Holt, Rinehart and Winston, 1982.

Vitz, Paul, and Arnold Glimcher. *Modern Art and Modern Science: The Parallel Analysis of Vision*. New York: Praeger Publishers, 1984.

Vogt, Paul. *Contemporary Painting*. New York: Harry N. Abrams, Inc., 1981.

Vyverberg, Henry. *The Living Tradition: Art, Music and Ideas in the Modern Western World*. New York: Harcourt, Brace and Jovanovich, 1978.

Walker, John A. *Art Since Pop*. London: Thames and Hudson, 1975.

Warner, Malcolm. *Portrait Painting*. Oxford: Phaidon Press Ltd., 1979.

Watrous, James. *A Century of American Printmaking, 1880–1980*. Madison, Wisconsin: The University of Wisconsin Press, 1984.

Wilmerding, John. *American Art*. New York: Penguin Books, 1976.

Wise, Kelly, ed. *Portrait: Theory*. New York: Lustrum Press, 1981.

ARTICLES

Adrian, Dennis. "Art Imitating Life in a Great Big Way." *Chicago Daily News*, 16–17 October 1976.

Alloway, Lawrence. "Art." *The Nation*. 1 May 1976.

Ammann, Jean-Christophe. "Realismus." *Flash Art* (May–July 1972): 50–52.

Andreae, Christopher. "Taking a Look." *Christian Science Monitor*, 19 March 1980.

"Art: La nouvelle coqueluch: L'hyperréalisme." *L'Express*, 30 October 1972.

Baker, Kenneth. "Leaving His Fingerprints." *Christian Science Monitor*, 12 August 1983.

Baldwin, Carl. "Le Penchant des peintres américains pour le Réalisme." *Connaissance des Arts* 254 (April 1973): 120.

———. "Realism: The American Mainstream." *Réalités* (November 1973): 42–51.

Bannard, Walter Darby. "New York Commentary." *Studio International* 183, no. 944 (May 1972): p. 255.

Bass, Ruth. "New York Reviews—Chuck Close (The Whitney Museum of American Art)" *ARTnews* 80, no. 9 (November 1981): 189.

Beamguard, Bud. "Close, Zucker, and Artschwager." *Artweek* 2 October 1976.

Berenson, Ruth. "Plight of Realism Today: Exhibition at the Whitney Museum." *National Review*, 5 May 1970.

Blau, Douglas. "Artists by Artists." *Arts* 54, no. 6 (February 1980): 12.

Borden, Lizzie. "Cosmologies." *Artforum* 11, no. 2 (October, 1972): 45–50.

———. "Reviews." *Artforum* 12, no. 2 (October 1973).

Bourdon, David. "Art: American Painting Regains Its Vital Signs." *Village Voice*, 17 March 1975.

———. "Beuys Will Be Beuys, Beckmann is Beckmann," *Village Voice*, 28 April 1975.

———. "Chuck Close: Portraits," *Vogue* (January 1980): 27.

———. "Redrawing the Lines of Drawing," *Village Voice*, 17 January 1977.

———. "Time Means Nothing to a Realist," *Village Voice*, 16 May 1977.

Bremer, Nina. "The New York Art Scene: Realism Today." *Revista de Arte, The Art Review* (September 1970): 3–7.

Brunelle, Al. "Reviews: Chuck Close." *ARTnews* 72, no. 4 (April 1973): 73.

Canaday, John. "Art: Miro's Joy and Verne/Chuck Close." *The New York Times*, 22 October 1973.

———. "Painters Who Put the World in Focus," *Smithsonian* (October 1981): 68–77.

Casademont, Joan. "Close Portraits." *Artforum* 20, no. 2 (October 1981): 74.

Cavaliere, Barbara. "Arts Reviews—Chuck Close." *Arts* 52, no. 1 (September 1977): 22.

———. "Arts Reviews—Chuck Close." *Arts* 54, no. 6 (February 1980): 33.

Cebulski, Frank. "Close to Photography." *Artweek*, 17 April 1982.

Chase, Linda. "Connotation of Denotation." *Arts* 48, no. 5 (February 1974): 38–41.

Chase, Linda, and Ted McBurnett. "Fiches-Chuck Close." *Opus International* 44/45 (1973): 40–41.

———. "Recycling Reality." *The Art Gallery Magazine*, October 1973: 75–82.

———. "Photo-Realism: Post Modernist Illusionism," *Art International* 20, no. 3/4 (March/April 1976).

"Chuck Close: Asket mit Pistole," *Der Spiegel*, 4 December 1972: 162–63.

Close, Chuck. "The Art of Portraiture in the Words of Four New York Artists." *The New York Times*, 31 October 1976.

———. "New York in the Eighties: A Symposium." *The New Criterion* (Summer 1986): 12–14.

———. *The Paris Review* 75 (Spring 1975): n. pag.

Coleman, A. D. "From Today Painting is Dead," *Camera 35* (July 1974): 34–38.

Collins, Nancy. "Eye View." *Women's Wear Daily*, 22 September 1972.

Cottingham, Jane. "An Interview with Chuck Close," *American Artist* 47, no. 490 (May 1983): 62–67, 102–5.

Danoff, I. Michael. "Chuck Close's Linda." *Arts* 57, no. 5 (January 1983): 110–11.

Davis, Douglas. "Art is Unnecessary, Or Is It?": Documenta 5 at the Friericianum Museum, Kassel, West Germany," *Newsweek*, 17 July 1972: 68–69.

———. "Nosing Out Reality." *Newsweek*, 14 August 1971: 58.

———. "Art without Limits." *Newsweek*, 24 December 1973: 68–74.

———. "The Return of the Nude." *Newsweek*, 1 September 1986: 78–79.

———. "Return of the Real: 22 Realists on View at New York's Whitney." *Newsweek*, 23 February 1970: 105.

deAk, Edit. "Photographic Realism." *Art-Rite* 9 (Spring 1975): 15.

Derfner, Phyllis. "New York Reviews." *Art International* 19, no. 6 (June 1975): 67.

———. "Reviews and Previews." *ARTnews* 70, no. 9 (January 1972): 12.

Diamonstein, Barbaralee. "Chuck Close: I'm Some Kind of a Slow-Motion Cornball." *ARTnews* 79, no. 6 (Summer 1980): 112–16.

———, and Thomas Hess. *American Photographer* 6, no. 2 (February 1981): 33.

"Die Kasseler Seh-Schule." *Der Stern* 36 (August 1972): 20–23.

Donhoff, Marion Graffin. "Die Nabelschau von Kassel." *Zeit* 9, no. 31 (August 1972).

Dyckes, William. "A One-Man Print Show by Chuck Close at MoMA." *Arts* 47, no. 3 (December/January 1973): 73.

———. "The Photo as Subject: The Paintings of Chuck Close." *Arts* 48, no. 5 (February 1974): 29–33. Reprinted in Battcock, Gregory, ed., *Super Realism: A Critical Anthology*. New York: 1975.

Elderfeld, John. "Whitney Annual." *Art in America* 60, no. 3. (May 1972): 29.

Ellenzweig, Allan. "Portrait Painting 1970–1975." *Arts* 49, no. 7 (March 1975): 13–14.

Feaver, William. "ARS '74/Helsinki." *Art International* 18, no. 5 (May 1974): 38–39.

ffrench-frazier, Nina. "New York Reviews—Chuck Close." *ARTnews* 76, no. 8 (October 1977): 130.

Flash Art (Documenta Issue) 76/77 (July/August 1977).

"Flashback su Kassel." *Flash Art* (September–October 1972): 16.

Gardner, Paul. "Confessions of a Plaintain Chip Eater or Artists Are Just Like the Rest of Us." *ARTnews* 80, no. 1 (January 1981): 137.

Gassiot-Talabot, Gerald. "Documenta V: Une Imposture sur 1'image?", *XX Siècle* 34, no. 39 (December 1972): 125–29.

———. "Le Choc des 'Réalismes.' " *XX Siècle* 42 (June 1974): 29.

Genauer, Emily. "Art '72: The Picture is Brighter." *The New York Post*, 31 December 1971.

Gibson, Eric. "Thinking About the Seventies." *The New Criterion* 3, no. 9 (May 1985): 45, 47, 48.

Gilmour, Par. "Photo-Realism." *Arts Review*, 21 April 1973: 249.

Glueck, Grace. "Artist Chuck Close: 'I Wanted to Make Images That Knock Your Socks Off!' " *The New York Times*, 10 June 1981.

———. "Drawing Show All-Star Cast." *The New York Times*, 23 March 1970.

———. "The 20th Century Artists Most Admired by Other Artists." *ARTnews* 76, no. 9 (November 1977): 82.

Gold, Barbara. "Art Notes: New Techniques Enough?" *Baltimore Sun*, 11 April 1976.

Goodyear, Frank H., Jr. "American Realism Since 1960: Beyond the 'Perfect Green Pea.' " *Portfolio* 3, no. 6 (November/December 1981): 72–81.

Greenwood, Mark. "Toward a Definition of Realism: Reflections on the Rothmans Exhibition," *Artscanada* 24, no. 210/211 (December 1976/January 1977): 6–23.

Gruen, John. "Museums and Galleries: It's Done with Mirrors." *New York Magazine*, 23 March 1970: 50.

Grundberg, Andy. "20 x 24 at Light." *Art in America* 68, no. 2 (February 1980): 133–34.

———. "Chuck Close at Pace/MacGill," *Art in America* 73, no. 5 (May 1985): 174–75.

———. "A Big Show That's About Something Larger Than Style." *The New York Times*, 23 February 1986.

Hagen, Charles. "Chuck Close/Pace/MacGill." *Artforum* 23, no. 8 (April 1985): 96–97.

———. "Reviews." *Artforum* 23, no. 8 (April 1985): 96.

Harshman, Barbara. "An Inverview with Chuck Close." *Arts* 52, no. 10 (June 1978): 142–45.

———. "Grids." *Arts* 53, no. 6 (February 1979): 4.

———. "Photo-Realist Printmaking." *Arts* 53, no. 6 (February 1979): 17.

Hartman, Rose. "Close Encounters." *American Photographer* 14, no. 4 (April 1985): 8.

Henry, Gerrit. "A Realist Twin Bill." *ARTnews* 72, no. 1 (January 1973): 26–28.

———. "Artist and the Face: A Modern American Sampling." *Art in America* 63, no. 1 (January 1975): 41.

———. "The Real Thing." *Art International* 16, no. 6–7 (Summer 1972): 87–91.

Hess, Thomas B. "Art: Americans in Paris." *New York Magazine*, 18 July 1977: 50–52.

———. "Art: Up Close with Richard, Philip, Nancy, and Klaus." *New York Magazine*, 30 May 1977: 95–97.

Hill, Richard. "The Technologies of Vision." *Art Magazine* 6, no. 19 (Fall 1974): 10.

Hoelterhoff, Manuela. "Close-Ups by Close." *The Wall Street Journal*, 17 April 1981.

Hudson, Andrew. "Washington Letter." *Art International* 19, no. 6 (June 1975): 94.

Hughes, Robert. "An Omnivorous and Literal Dependence." *Arts* 48, vol. 9 (June 1974): 25–29.

———. "Blowing Up the Closeup." *Time*, 23 May 1977: 92.

———. "Close, Closer, Closest." *Time*, 27 April 1981: 60.

———. "Last Salon: Biannual Exhibition at New York's Whitney Museum." *Time*, 12 February 1973: 46.

———. "The Realist as Corn God." *Time*, 31 January 1972: 50–55.

Joaido, Philip, and Gilles Neret. "Les Américains: toujours le plus forts." *Connaissance des Arts* 333 (November 1979): 102–9.

Johnson, F. H. "American Art of 20th Century: Allen Memorial Art Museum." *Apollo* 103, no. 168 (February 1976): 135.

Jordan, Jim. "A Question of Scale." *Artweek*, 13 July 1985: 10.

Karp, Ivan. "Rent is the Only Reality, or the Hotel Instead of the Hymn." *Arts* 46, no. 3 (December 1971): 50.

Kelley, Mary Lou. "Pop-Art Inspired Objective Realism." *Christian Science Monitor*, 1 April 1974.

Kertess, Klaus. "Figuring It Out." *Artforum* 19, no. 3 (November 1980): 30–35.

Kramer, Hilton. "Art: The Fascination of Portraits." *The New York Times*, 22 October 1976.

———. "Art Season: A New Realism Emerges." *The New York Times*, 21 December 1971.

———. "Art View: Chuck Close—In Flight from the Realist Impulse." *The New York Times*, 4 November 1979.

———. "Art View: Today's Avant-Garde Artists Have Lost the Power to Shock." *The New York Times*, 16 November 1980.

———. "Back to Beaubourg: A Modern Exposition Palace." *The New York Times*, 1 July 1979.

———. "Chuck Close's Break with Photography." *The New York Times*, 19 April 1981.

———. "MoMA Reopened: The Museum of Modern Art in the Post Modern Era." *The New Criterion* (Summer 1984): 34.

———. "Portraiture: The Living Art." *Bazaar* 3232 (March 1981): 14, 28.

———. "Reviews: Chuck Close." *The New York Times*, 26 April 1975.

———. "Stealing the Modernist Fire." *The New York Times*, 26 December 1971.

Kurtz, Bruce. "Documenta 5: A Critical Preview." *Arts* 46, no. 8 (Summer 1972): 41.

Kurtz, Stephan A., "Reviews and Previews." *ARTnews* 68:4 (Summer 1969): 12.

Kutner, Janet. "The Visceral Aesthetic of a New Decade's Art." *Arts* 51, no. 4 (December 1976): 100–103.

Larson, Kay. "America's Special Light." *New York Magazine* 16, no. 12 (March 1983): 59–60

———. "Art," *New York Magazine*, 11 May 1981: 75.

———. "Dead-End Realism." *New York Magazine*, 26 October 1981: 94–95.

Lascault, Gilbert. "Auteur de quelques portraits." *XX Siècle* 44 (June 1975): 123–31.

Levin, Kim. "Chuck Close: Decoding the Image." *Arts* 52, no. 10 (June 1978): 146–49.

———. "The Newest Realism: A Synthetic Slice of Life." *Opus International* 44/45 (June 1973): 28–37.

Lord, B. "Whitney Museum's 22 Realists Exhibition." *Artscanada* 27, no. 3 (June 1970): 11.

Loring, John. "Photographic Illusionist Prints." *Arts* 48, no. 5 (February 1974): 42–43.

Lucie-Smith, Edward. "The Neutral Style." *Art and Artists* 10, no. 5 (August 1975): 6–15.

Marandel, J. Patrice. "Expositions à la Bykert Gallery," *Art International* 14, no. 5 (May 1970): 86.

———. "The Deductive Image: Notes on Some Figurative Painters." *Art International* 15, no. 7 (September 1971): 58–61.

Marvel, Bill. "Saggy Nudes? Giant Heads? Make Way for Superrealism." *The National Observer*, 29 January 1972: 22.

Meisel, Louis K. "Fifteen Years of Photo-Realism." *Horizon* 23, no. 11 (November 1980): 59.

Mellow, James. "Largest Mezzotint by Close Shown." *The New York Times*, 13 January 1973.

Melville, Robert. "The Photograph as Subject." *Architectural Review* 153, no. 915 (May 1973): 329–33.

Miotke, Anne. "Close Dot Drawings." *Mid-West Art* (March 1976): 11, 20.

McClain, Matthew. "Realist Blockbuster Stirs Controversy: Interview with Curator Frank Goodyear." *The New Art Examiner* 9, no. 3 (December 1981): 7–27.

Naimer, Lucille. "The Whitney Annual." *Arts* 46, no. 5, (March 1972): 54.

Nemser, Cindy. "An Interview with Chuck Close." *Artforum* 8, no. 5 (January 1970): 51–55.

———. "Close Up Vision: Representational Art—Part II." *Arts* 46, no. 7 (May 1972): 47–48.

———. "Fotografiet Som Sandhed" (Interview with Chuck Close). *Louisiana Revy* 13, no. 13 (February 1973): 30–33.

———. "In the Museums." *Arts* 44 no. 2 (February, 1970): 54.

———. "Presenting Charles Close." *Art in America* 58, no. 1 (January 1970): 98–101.

———. "Reviews in the Galleries." *Arts* 43, no. 8 (Summer 1969): 58.

Nochlin, Linda. "The Realist Criminal and the Abstract Law." *Art in America* 61, no. 5 (September 1973): 54–61.

Patton, Phil. "SuperRealism: A Critical Anthology." *Artforum* 14, no. 5 (January 1976): 52–54.

Peppiatt, Michael. "Paris." *Art International* 18, no. 4 (April 1974): 52, 74–75.

Perreault, John. "Abstract Heads." *Soho Weekly News*, 19 May 1977.

———. "A Lollapalozza of a Mishmash." *Village Voice*, 10 February 1972.

———. "A New Turn of the Screw: Drawings by Chuck Close." *Village Voice*, 1 November 1973: 34.

———. "Chuck Close." *Village Voice*, 12 March 1970: 15–16.

———. "Encounters of the Close Kind." *Soho Weekly News*, 29 April 1981.

———. "Get Back." *Village Voice*, 19 February 1970.

———. "Paperworks." *American Craft* 42, no. 4 (August/September 1982): 2–7.

———. "Photorealing in the Years." *Soho Weekly News*, 20 October 1981.

———. "Photo-Realist Principles." *American Art Review* 4, no. 6 (November 1978): 108–11, 141.

———. "Post-Photo Realism." *Soho Weekly News*, 22 November 1979.

———. "Realisms." *Art Express* 2, no. 2 (March/April 1982): 34–38.

———. "Realistically Speaking. . . ." *Village Voice*, 14 December 1972.

———. "Reports, Forecasts, Surprises and Prizes." *Village Voice*, 6 January 1972.

———. "Return of the Real." *Village Voice*, 23 February 1970: 105.

———. "The Hand was Colossal But Small." *Village Voice*, 23 March 1972: 72.

———. "The Year in Pictures (Among Other Things)." *Soho Weekly News*, 12 January 1982.

Peters, Lisa. "Reviews: Chuck Close." *Arts* 57, no. 9 (May 1983): 52.

Poirier, Maurice. "Chuck Close." *ARTnews* 85, no. 5 (May 1986): 127.

Pozzi, Lucio. "Super Realisti U.S.A." *Bolaffiarte* 18 (March 1972): 54–63.

Raddatz, Von Fritz J. "Amerika auf der Suche nach seinen Wurzeln." *Die Zeit*, 26 (December 1980).

Ratcliff, Carter. "New York Letter." *Art International* 16, no. 2 (February 1972): 54–55.

———. "New York Letter." *Art International* 21, no. 4 (July/August 1977): 78–79.

———. "New York Letter." *Art International* 25, no. 1/2 (January 1982): 116–17.

———. "Making It in the Art World: A Climber's Guide." *New York Magazine*, 27 November 1978: 61–67.

———. "Reviews and Previews." *ARTnews* 69, no. 2 (April 1970): 16.

———. "22 Realists Exhibit at the Whitney."*Art International* 14, no.3 (April 1970):67.

Raynor, Vivien. "Chuck Close." *The New York Times*, 28 February 1986.

Rice, Shelley. "Image Making." *Soho Weekly News*, 24 May 1979.

Rose, Barbara. "Real, Realer, Realist." *New York Magazine*, 31 January 1972: 50.

———. "Two Women: Real and More Real." *Vogue*, May 1973: 83.

Rosenberg, Harold. "Inquiry '72: On the Edge, Documenta 5." *The New Yorker*, 9 September 1972: 75.

Russell, John. "Art: Portraiture by 31 Painters." *The New York Times*, 25 January 1975.

———. "Big Heads That Satisfy." *The New York Times*, 6 May 1977.

———. "Gallery View." *The New York Times*, 3 June 1979.

———. "Portrait Show at Whitney Downtown." *The New York Times*, 30 November 1974.

Ryan, David. "Two Contemporary Acquisitions for Minneapolis." *The Minneapolis Institute of Arts Bulletin* 58: 82–83.

Sager, Peter. "Neue Formen des Realismus." *Magazin Kunst* 44, (1971): 2512–16.

Sandback, Amy Baker, and Ingrid Sischy. "A Progression by Chuck Close: Who's Afraid of Photography?" *Artforum* 22, no. 9 (May 1984): 50.

Schjeldahl, Peter. "Realism on the Comeback Trail." *The Village Voice*, 11–17 November 1981.

Schwartz, Ellen. "New York Reviews: Chuck Close at Pace." *ARTnews* 79, no. 1 (January 1980): 157.

Seitz, William C. "The Real and the Artificial: Painting of the New Environment." *Art in America* 60, no. 6 (November/December 1972): 58–72.

Seldis, Henry J. "Art Review: Appearance and Beyond." *Los Angeles Times*, 12 January 1976.

———. "Art Review: Chuck Close Work Shown." *Los Angeles Times*, 4 October 1971.

Simon, Joan, "Close Encounters." *Art in America* 68, no. 2 (February 1980): 81–83.

Shapiro, Michael. "Changing Variables: Chuck Close and His Prints." *The Print Collector's Newsletter* 9, no. 3 (July/August) pp. 69–73.

Shirley, David L. "More Real Than Real." *The New York Times*, 6 August 1978.

Smith, Roberta. "34th Biennial of Contemporary Painting." *Artforum* 13, no. 9 (May 1975): 72.

Spear, Athena. "Reflections on Close, Cooper and Jenny: Three Young Americans at Oberlin." *Arts* 44, no. 7 (May 1970): 44–47.

Spector, Stephen. "The Super Realists." *Architectural Digest* (November/December 1974): 84–89

Stevens, Mark. "Close Up Close." *Newsweek*, 23 May 1977.

———. "Revival of Realism." *Newsweek*, 7 June 1982.

Stubbs, Ann. "Audrey Flack." *Soho Weekly News*, 4 April 1974.

Szeeman, Harold. "Documenta 5." *L'Art Vivant* 25 (November 1971): 4–7.

Tallmer, Jerry. "All Equal on the Grid." *The New York Post*, 27 October 1979.

"Three Realists: Close, Estes, Raffael." *Connoisseur* 186, no. 748 (June 1974): 142–43.

Tully, Judd. "The Paper Chase." *Portfolio* 5, no. 3 (May/June 1983): 78–85.

Wallach, Amei. "Looking Closer at Chuck Close." *Newsday*, 19 April 1981.

Walsh, Mike E. "Chuck Close: Realist or Minimalist?" *Artweek*, 18 October 1975.

Wasmuth, Ernst. "La Révolte des Réalistes." *Connaissance des Arts* 246 (June 1972): 118–23.

Wasserman, Emily. "Group Show/Bykert Gallery." *Artforum* 8, no. 1 (September 1969): 61.

Wilson, William. "Documenta 6 More Moving Than Good" *Los Angeles Times*, 3 July 1977.

———. "The Chilly Charms of Close." *Los Angeles Times*, 8 June 1981.

Wolff, Theodore F. "Huge, Photographically Exact Paintings of Faces That Signify . . . What?" *Christian Science Monitor* (West ed.), 29 April 1981.

Wolmer, Denise. "In the Galleries." *Arts* 46, no. 4 (February 1972): 58.

Worts, Melinda, "New Editions" *ARTnews* 81, no. 4 (April 1982): 102.

Die Zeit. (Documenta Issue) 31, no. 4 (August 1972): 4–15.

Zimmer, William. "Art Reviews." *Arts* 49, no. 10 (June 1975): 8.

INDEX OF WORKS